THE SERMON
on the
MOUNT

THE SERMON
on the
MOUNT

JIMMY SWAGGART

JIMMY SWAGGART MINISTRIES
P.O. Box 262550 | Baton Rouge, Louisiana 70826-2550
www.jsm.org

ISBN 978-1-941403-41-9

09-153 | COPYRIGHT © 2018 Jimmy Swaggart Ministries®

18 19 20 21 22 23 24 25 26 27 / TS / 10 9 8 7 6 5 4 3 2 1

TABLE OF CONTENTS

THE SERMON
on the
MOUNT

INTRODUCTION

INTRODUCTION

JESUS BEGAN HIS MINISTRY with a sermon on the mount (Mat., Chpts. 5-7) and closed it with a sermon on the mount (Mat., Chpt. 24).

The conclusion of His ministry was on the Mount of Olives, which is in Jerusalem. The Sermon on the Mount where He began His ministry is not specified in the Word of God. The Bible simply says, *"He went up into a mountain,"* without saying which one it was (Mat. 5:1).

However, it is strongly believed (and more than likely is correct) that this mountain was beside the Sea of Galilee. I have been there many times. The top of the mountain is flat, which can accommodate a lot of people. Of the hundreds and possibly even thousands who were there that day, I wonder how many of them realized that as He gave this sermon, it was a compendium of the entirety of the plan of God. In other words, it was what God expects of mankind, and what mankind can only be in Christ. Actually, this sermon began with the Beatitudes. If one wants to know how to live, one need only read the sermon. However, let me emphasize it again: within our own strength and ability, it is impossible to obey the message given. It simply cannot be done. Due to the fall, the clinging vines of that catastrophe guarantee defeat. Yet, it can be done, but it is only in Christ and only because of what He did for us at the Cross.

THE PROPHET

From the time of Malachi to Christ, a period of nearly 450 years, other than the voice of John the Baptist, the forerunner of Christ, Israel did not hear the voice of a single prophet. No doubt, with the voice of John the Baptist, a fresh wind began to blow in Israel, and in truth, for the entirety of the world. The reason was that John's voice would herald the coming of the One of whom the prophets of old had spoken, and we speak of the Lord Jesus Christ.

Accordingly, the Holy Spirit would use Matthew, a publican, to first herald the greatest event to date in the annals of human history. The honor and distinction of such cannot be adequately portrayed by mere verbiage. By using Matthew in this high and honored position, one can only proclaim such as an act of the grace of God. As well, we must quickly say that Matthew readily portrayed virtually the beginning of his book by cataloging the Sermon on the Mount.

THE MESSAGE OF CHRIST

To differentiate between the messages given by our Lord in His three and a half years of public ministry, it is impossible to exhaust the potential of that which He gave to the world. However the Sermon on the Mount probably says it better than anything else. I pray that in our efforts, we will be able to somehow convey what the Holy Spirit intended. If so, then your time spent reading this book will be well worthwhile. I pray that the Holy Spirit will make it so real that it will be as though you were standing on that mountain that day when Jesus began to speak to the great crowd. They had never heard anything like it. The messages of the scribes, the priests, and the Pharisees were dry and stodgy with no life. However, when Christ spoke, the Holy Spirit took His words straight to the hearts of the people. It goes without saying that He experienced the anointing of the Holy Spirit to speak to the people as no other human being ever had—not even the great prophets of old. Consequently, the people who heard this message would never be the same again.

I trust that in some way, the Holy Spirit will so anoint our words that you will be blessed accordingly. If so, then our efforts will be worthwhile, and your time spent perusing this book will not be wasted.

Oh Zion haste, your mission high fulfilling,
To tell all the world that God is Light,
That He who made all nations is not willing
One soul should perish, lost in shades of night.

Behold how many thousands still are lying,
Bound in the darksome prison house of sin,
With none to tell them of the Saviour's dying,
Or of the life He died for them to win.

Proclaim to every people, tongue, and nation,
That God, in whom they live and move is love:
Tell how He stooped to save His lost creation,
And died on earth that man might live above.

Give of your sons to bear the message glorious;
Give of your wealth to speed them on their way,
Pour out your soul for them in prayer victorious,
And all you spend Jesus will repay.

He comes again: Oh Zion, ere you meet Him,
Make known to every heart His saving grace;
Let none whom He has ransomed fail to greet Him,
Through your neglect, unfit to see His face.

THE SERMON

on the

MOUNT

CHAPTER 1

RIGHTEOUSNESS

RIGHTEOUSNESS

"AND SEEING THE MULTITUDES, He went up into a mountain: and when He was set, His disciples came unto Him" (Mat. 5:1).

THE MULTITUDE

The phrase, *"And seeing the multitudes,"* portrays the beginning of the ministry of our Lord. Considering the tremendous miracles, healings, and deliverances, there was no reason for Israel not to know who He was! Daniel had prophesied basically as to the time of His appearance, which, no doubt, the scribes studied intently. Considering that such a miracle, at least in such a wholesale manner, had never been brought about by the prophets of the past, there was no excuse regarding His identification (Dan. 9:25-26). Consequently, the multitudes came for two reasons:

1. The miracles and healings He performed.

2. The gracious words that proceeded out of His mouth.

OPPOSITION

Sadly, at the conclusion of His ministry, the crowds would thin out dramatically, and that was despite His miracle-working power (Jn. 6:66). Their leaving was for two reasons:

1. It was because of the things He taught: *"Except you eat the flesh of the Son of Man, and drink His blood, you have no life in you"* (Jn. 6:53). Of course, He was speaking of His coming death on the Cross of Calvary and the shedding of His life's blood. To be saved, individuals would have to believe in Him and what He did for us at the Cross.

2. The last year of His ministry, the crowds thinned out considerably because of the tremendous opposition by the Pharisees. This actually included, as well, the Sadducees and the Herodians, with their threatening excommunication for anyone who followed Him (Jn. 9:22). To be excommunicated from the synagogue meant being cut off from all Jewish life, and I mean *all* Jewish life.

Considering His miracles, it is almost unbelievable that the people would allow their religious leaders to dictate their choice, but they did. Such is religion!

The phrase, *"He went up into a mountain,"* does not say which mountain, but it is thought to be a small mountain near the Sea of Galilee. More than likely, that is correct.

The phrase, *"And when He was set, His disciples came unto Him,"* refers to Him sitting down when He talked, with the word *disciples* referring to any and all who closely followed Him at that particular time.

THE TEACHING OF OUR LORD

"And He opened His mouth, and taught them, saying" (Mat. 5:2).

"And He opened His mouth," indicates that the words spoken were not the utterances of spur of the moment, but instead, a carefully thought-out message of purpose and will.

The phrase, *"And taught them, saying,"* begins the greatest moment of spiritual and scriptural instruction that had ever been given in the history of mankind. It is said that men marvelled at the gracious words that proceeded out of His mouth, and rightly so. He was anointed by the Holy Spirit as no other human being had ever been anointed.

Two sermons, both of which were delivered on mountains, opened and closed the Lord's public ministry. The first, as here recorded, was probably delivered on a mountain near Capernaum, and the last was delivered upon the Mount of Olivet near Jerusalem (Mat., Chpt. 24).

The theme of each was the kingdom from the heavens—its moral characteristics in the first discourse; its fortunes and its future in the second.

BLESSED

"Blessed are the poor in spirit: for theirs is the kingdom of heaven" (Mat. 5:3).

The word *blessed* begins that which is commonly called the Beatitudes.

The word *blessed,* as used in the Beatitudes, is somewhat different than the word *blessed* as used in the Psalms; however, there are similarities.

The *"blessed are"* statements in the Psalms describe human attitudes or actions that lead to blessing.

The Beatitudes also look at human attitudes; however, Jesus moved beyond the Old Testament covenant. He made the startling statement that God's kingdom is a present kingdom, and that His blessed ones already know (are happy with) a unique joy, which comes from living in that kingdom. The word *blessed,* as Jesus used it in the Beatitudes, means "to be happy," which is derived not from external sources but from internal sources and speaks of the joy of the Lord. In the Old Testament, the word *blessed* looked forward to something that could be achieved if certain things were done. Now, because of the Lord and what He has done for us, and I speak of the Cross, blessing is a present fact.

THE CROSS

The modern church understands somewhat the Cross of Christ as it refers to salvation but almost none at all as it refers to sanctification. And yet, as far as teaching is concerned, far more teaching is given in the New Testament regarding the Cross of Christ and sanctification, in other words, how we live for God, than anything else. The church, for the most part, has so abandoned the Cross in the last few decades that it doesn't know anymore, where it has been, where it is, or where it is going.

These Beatitudes describe the inner experience of the believer, who, in comforting others, etc., knows the supernatural comfort provided by God and senses the healing touch of God that rests on those who mourn.

THE OLD TESTAMENT

The Old Testament type of blessing, as stated, describes the path that leads to God's blessing. Jesus describes that blessing itself. In effect, Christ states that God's blessing comes to us in all our circumstances and makes us fortunate and blessed, no matter how others may view our lives.

However, the Beatitudes express a gospel that is totally contrary to much of that being taught presently in that which I refer to as "a false message," etc.

Jesus portrays an experience of the kingdom's inner riches amid external poverty and trial, which presents a divine paradox. It is so important that the reader must allow us to say it again: "That which Christ gave as the very foundation of the Christian experience does not by any means guarantee a life free of trials, tests, or other vicissitudes of life, but does guarantee inner riches, which produce happiness based on joy, despite the external circumstances that sometimes are not favorable."

In fact, without going into detail, the Apostle Paul is a perfect example.

As should be obvious, this is true Christianity and is a far cry from much that is promoted presently.

THE POOR IN SPIRIT

The phrase, *"Blessed are the poor in spirit,"* constitutes the opening recorded phrase of Christ's public teaching ministry. As this is the first utterance, it is done so with design and purpose. The phrase, *"Poor in spirit,"* means to be conscious of moral and spiritual poverty, which struck at the very heart of Israel's present situation (which was self-righteousness) and the very heart of the problems of all for all time. Actually, this first beatitude is the sum and substance of the entirety of Christ's teaching. Poverty of spirit stands in contrast to self-sufficiency (Rev. 3:17).

In other words, *"poor in spirit"* means that the individual understands that he personally is morally bankrupt, meaning that there is nothing about him, and I mean nothing, that is appealing to the Lord. He is totally bereft and totally bankrupt of all that is good, at least as God defines goodness. Once he understands this, then the Lord can begin to move in such a person's heart and life and change that heart and life to something that is good. To be sure, this is the problem of the entirety of the world and for all time. Men refuse to admit what they really are, which is spiritual bankruptcy of every description. It is only when they do admit this, understand this, and throw themselves on the mercy and grace of God that the Lord can begin to change their hearts and their lives.

SELF-RIGHTEOUSNESS

This first beatitude strikes at the very heart of man's problem of self-righteousness and self-sufficiency, which came about as a result of the fall in the garden of Eden. Therefore, the very first word strikes at the very heart of man's basic problem, a problem, as we have stated, so anchored in the human psyche that only the power of God can affect its direction.

As this phrase, *"Poor in spirit,"* sets the stage for Christ's ministry, we find His teaching constant in this regard throughout His ministry. For instance, the parable of the Pharisee and the publican, as given in Luke 18:9-14, is an excellent example.

The former extolled his goodness, while the latter extolled his moral poverty.

Jesus said that the latter *"went down to his house justified rather than the other."* He then went on to say, *"For every one who exalts himself shall be abased; and he who humbles himself shall be exalted"* (Lk. 18:14).

THE KINGDOM OF HEAVEN

The phrase, *"For theirs is the kingdom of heaven,"* as given in this first beatitude, refers to the fact that such were already in the kingdom. Even though this kingdom of heaven was not then realized materially or physically because of Israel's rejection of Christ, still, it was realized spiritually. It continues to be so today in a thousand times greater way than ever because of the Cross. And yet, those who are in the kingdom are almost altogether Gentiles.

Nevertheless, at the second coming, it will be realized materially, physically, and spiritually. Consequently, it will also be geographical, i.e., covering the entirety of the world. In other words, the kingdom of heaven, which actually means, "The kingdom from the heavens," will then be brought down to earth. In fact, it could have been done some 2,000 years ago but for the fact that Israel rejected the King, who is the Lord Jesus Christ. Respecting that, the world has been made subject to war, bloodshed, criminal activity, poverty, superstition, etc., from then until now because of Israel's rejection of Christ.

THEY WHO MOURN

"Blessed are they who mourn: for they shall be comforted" (Mat. 5:4).

The Cross of Christ, so to speak, began in the mind of the Godhead from before the foundation of the world. In other words, through foreknowledge, God knew He would create the universe, this planet, and man, and He knew that man would fall. It was then decided by the Godhead that man would be redeemed by God becoming man and going to the Cross, hence, the incarnation (I Pet. 1:18-20).

In other words, the Cross was the very reason for God becoming man.

Despite the fall and being driven from the garden, the Lord gave Adam and Eve, and all who would follow, a means by which they could still have forgiveness of sins and communion with Him. It would be by virtue of the slain lamb offered in sacrifice, which would be symbolic of the One who was to come—the Lord Jesus Christ. However, please understand, the sacrificial system, which typified the Cross of Christ, was God's way, and His only way.

PERSONAL MORAL POVERTY

The second beatitude, *"Blessed are they who mourn: for they shall be comforted,"* dovetails the first because it means to grieve because of one's personal moral poverty. All of us must understand, even those who are the closest to the Lord, that, still, we continue on a constant basis to *"come short of the glory of God"* (Rom. 3:23). This means that the Bible most definitely does not teach sinless perfection; however, it most definitely does teach that sin is not to have dominion over us, meaning to control us (Rom. 6:14).

No matter how holy we may think we are and, in fact, no matter how holy we actually are, without the Cross of Christ, none of us would have any standing whatsoever before the Lord. In other words, while Jesus Christ is the source of all things we receive from God, the Cross of Christ is the means, and the only means, by which all of these things are given to us, whatever they might be.

WERE IT NOT FOR THE CROSS ...

Were it not for the Cross, the Lord could not even look at us, much less have communion with us. When we speak of the Cross, of course, I'm sure you realize that we aren't speaking of the wooden beam on which Jesus died. Rather, we are speaking of what He there did, which was to atone for all sin and also defeat Satan, every fallen angel, and every demon spirit (Heb. 10:12; Col. 2:14-15).

So, as it regards this constant coming short of the glory of God, no matter how hard we try otherwise, if we truly know the Lord, we mourn over that, even as we should.

While my position and your position are perfect in Christ because of our faith in Him and what He did for you and me, still, that doesn't mean that our condition is perfect. In fact, it is the work of the Holy Spirit, which is a lifelong project, to bring our condition up to our position. The truth is, such will never be completely done, but all of us can most definitely be drawn closer than we presently are, and it ought to be that every day draws us a little bit closer.

A PERSONAL ANSWER

Someone asked me the other day as to exactly how they could tell they were close to God. I thought for a moment, realizing that most of us are prone to answer in respect to all of the things we do concerning Bible study, church attendance, the giving of money to the work of God, witnessing to people about the Lord, etc.

Of course, these things are important, even very important. However, that is the very thing the Pharisee extolled in Luke, Chapter 18.

Even though commendable, and at least in most cases, certainly approved by the Lord, still, it is no sign of that which speaks of closeness to God.

The answer I believe the Lord gave me, which was startling even to me, was in this vein: "The more the Holy Spirit is correcting us, the closer we are to God."

Sometime back, after seeking the Lord incessantly, drawing nearer to Him, and sensing the result of that nearness, I asked the Lord in prayer if such was the case (the constant correcting by the Holy Spirit), why did I feel so undone at times in my spirit.

THE LIGHT

The answer was immediately forthcoming:

The Lord said, "The further away one is from the light, the less the flaws show up. The closer one gets, the more the light exposes the flaws, stains, and inconsistencies."

The present attitude of too many Christians who extol their great place and position in Christ, and do so with much bravado, is totally contrary to that which Christ taught.

While it is certainly true that all believers have great place and station in Christ, still, this was given to us only by His grace and not at all because of our self-worthiness.

As a result, realizing what has been truly and wonderfully given to us and honestly observing our state of moral imperfection, it causes the true Christian to *"mourn,"* and rightly so. By that, we do not mean a mournful expression or attitude, but rather that we feel the weight of it all, and in our spirit, we do mourn over this.

This is that of which Paul was speaking when he said, *"For we who are in this tabernacle do groan, being burdened: not for that we would be unclothed, but clothed upon, that mortality might be swallowed up of life"* (II Cor. 5:4). In other words, we long for that glorified body, for then, there will be no more sin or failure.

COMFORTED

The phrase, *"For they shall be comforted,"* speaks of that which the Holy Spirit will give to those who properly evaluate their spiritual poverty.

Once again, this can only be done by the means of the Cross. Every believer on the face of the earth is either functioning under law or grace, which has always been the case. By law, we are referring to anything in which we place our faith—irrespective as to what it is—other than Christ and what He did for us at the Cross.

Sadly and regrettably, by not understanding the Cross of Christ as it regards our sanctification—how we live for God, how we overcome the world, the flesh, and the Devil—most Christians, and we speak of those who truly love the Lord, are, in fact, living under law.

As a result, there is a constant frustration in the heart and life of such a person. As well, there is a constant anger just beneath the surface that causes misery, to say the least. This means that such a person, although loving the Lord, is out of sync with the Lord, so to speak. God's way is the Cross of Christ. It is not law.

FAITH

Jesus Christ finished the law in every respect. In His life and living, He kept the law perfectly in word, thought, and deed. In other words, He never failed, not even one time. He addressed the broken law, of which all of us were guilty, by going to the Cross and offering Himself as a perfect sacrifice, which was accepted by the Lord. We are to have faith in that sacrifice, and have faith constantly in that sacrifice. With that being done, the Holy Spirit will help us to enjoy, as it is intended to be, this more abundant life (Jn. 10:10). Every person who is truly born again has more abundant life; however, the truth is, only a precious few are actually enjoying it—only the ones whose faith is properly placed. Then and only then is there comfort, and what a comfort it is!

I have personally been on both sides of this proverbial fence. Please believe me, I don't want to go back to that other side ever again. That side is nothing but failure; on the Cross side, there is nothing but victory (Rom. 6:1-14; 8:1-11; I Cor. 1:17-18, 23; 2:2). Let's say it this way:

- Without the Cross of Christ, there is no salvation.

- Without the Cross of Christ, there is no baptism with the Holy Spirit.

- Without the Cross of Christ, there is no divine healing.

- Without the Cross of Christ, there is no blessing.

BLESSED ARE THE MEEK

"Blessed are the meek: for they shall inherit the earth" (Mat. 5:5).

The *"meek"* are the opposite of the self-righteous and logically follow in order the *"poor in spirit"* and *"they who mourn."* In other words, the first two beatitudes guarantee the meekness.

Its general thrust is toward God, as all three of these beatitudes speak, but such will result in meekness toward men.

Therefore, meekness is not possible to those who are not *"poor in spirit"* or do not *"mourn"* over their spiritual poverty. The only personal thing that Jesus said of Himself was, *"I am meek and lowly in heart"* (Mat. 11:29).

Meekness is not weakness, but rather controlled strength.

When mentioning a godly soul, someone made mention of the fact, "They were so full of God because they were so empty of self."

The Greek word for meek is "praus" and pictures a humble, gentle attitude that maintains patience despite offenses and is untainted by vengefulness or malice.

CHRIST

A beautiful picture of this attitude as shown in Christ is found in I Peter 2:21-23: *"For even hereunto were you called:*

because Christ also suffered for us, leaving us an example, that we should follow His steps: Who did no sin, neither was guile found in His mouth: Who, when He was reviled, reviled not again; when He suffered, He threatened not; but committed Himself to Him who judges righteously."

THE CROSS OF CHRIST AND HUMILITY

Unless one properly understands the Cross of Christ as it regards our sanctification (in other words, how we live for God on a daily basis) and the great part that the Cross plays in all of this—which opens everything up to the Holy Spirit—I do not personally believe that such a person can know or understand meekness to any degree.

In other words, any meekness other than a proper understanding of the Cross is a man-devised meekness and is never that which God will recognize.

The following is taken from The Expositor's Study Bible:

Let nothing be done through strife or vainglory; but in lowliness of mind (meekness) *let each esteem other better than themselves* (which a correct viewpoint of the Cross will bring about). *Look not every man on his own things* (means to look only at one's own things)*, but every man also on the things of others* (an interest in the affairs of others). *Let this mind be in you* (refers to the self-emptying of Christ), *which was also in Christ Jesus* (portrays Christ as the supreme example): *Who, being in the form of God* (refers to Deity, which Christ always was), *thought it not robbery to be equal with God* (equality with God refers here to our Lord's co-participation with the other members of the Trinity in the expression of the divine essence)*:*

MADE HIMSELF OF NO REPUTATION

But made Himself of no reputation (instead of asserting His rights to the expression of the essence of Deity, our Lord waved His rights to that expression), *and took upon Him the form of a servant* (a bondslave), *and was made in the likeness of men* (presents the Lord entering into a new state of being when He became man; but Him becoming man did not exclude His position of Deity; while in becoming man, He laid aside the 'expression' of Deity, He never lost 'possession' of Deity)*: And being found in fashion as a man* (denotes Christ in men's eyes), *He humbled Himself* (He was brought low, but willingly)*, and became obedient unto death* (does not mean He became obedient to death; He was always the master of death; rather, He subjected Himself to death), *even the death of the Cross.* (This presents the character of His death as one of disgrace and degradation, which was necessary for men to be redeemed. This type of death alone would pay the terrible sin debt, and do so in totality) (Phil. 2:3-8).

Let me say it again: I do not feel that meekness to any degree is possible unless the believer understands the Cross of Christ relative to his everyday living for God. One might say that the Cross of Christ, among many other things, was the greatest example of meekness the world has ever known. Christ had the power to call down as many legions of angels as He needed, and was taunted by the Pharisees to do so, but never used that power, and thank God that He didn't.

HUNGER AND THIRST AFTER RIGHTEOUSNESS

"Blessed are they which do hunger and thirst after righteousness: for they shall be filled" (Mat. 5:6).

The phrase, *"Blessed are they which do hunger and thirst after righteousness,"* speaks of intense desire, even as a man starving for natural food. He must receive sustenance or else he will die.

Consequently, the idea is that if the seeker does not receive what he so hungrily desires (righteousness in this case), he will die.

Let us bring the Cross of Christ into this:

- The maturity of the believer is predicated solely upon his understanding of the Cross of Christ.

- The consecration of the believer is predicated solely upon his understanding of the Cross of Christ.

- The victory of the believer is predicated solely upon his understanding of the Cross of Christ.

THE POVERTY OF RIGHTEOUSNESS
IN THE HUMAN LIFE

The very idea of verse 6 proclaims the poverty of righteousness in the human life, which speaks of God's righteousness. This is one totally empty of all self-righteousness, realizing, as the previous beatitudes portray, that this is a commodity he does not have and cannot obtain through any self-worth or self-merit. It is one totally void of self-righteousness and is hungering for the righteousness of God.

This individual senses strongly his moral poverty, the absolute destitution of his own merit, and consequently, his desperate need for the righteousness of God, which can only be given by grace.

RIGHTEOUSNESS AND THE CROSS OF CHRIST

Man has no righteousness, at least that which God will recognize. Let me make this statement, and even though it is strong, it is true: Faith placed in anything other than the Cross of Christ, no matter how scriptural and wonderful it might be in its own right, always and without fail leads to self-righteousness. Even though it is a hard and strong statement, the truth is, the modern church is the most self-righteous church that has existed since the Reformation.

Why? It is because the modern church has absolutely no understanding of the Cross of Christ relative to life and living, which speaks of our everyday walk before God. It understands the Cross, at least to a certain extent, as it regards salvation; however, as the Cross applies to our everyday life and living, the modern church has absolutely no understanding whatsoever.

ABRAHAM, ISAAC, AND ISHMAEL

Please notice the following very carefully:

Pure and simple, Ishmael was a work of the flesh. It was the effort of Abraham and Sarah to "help God" bring a little boy child into the world, through whom the Redeemer would ultimately come, i.e., the incarnation, God becoming man. With Ishmael being a product of the flesh, he could not please God, as anything that man devises cannot please God.

Unless the Holy Spirit conceives the idea, gives birth to the idea, administers the idea, and empowers the idea, it is that which God can never recognize.

In other words, man, even the godliest, cannot bring forth anything out of his own brainpower, his own motivation, or his own talent and ability that God can use. He can only use that conceived and carried out by the Holy Spirit. This is something that man is very slow to learn. In fact, this problem began with Eve.

When Cain was born, Eve said, *"I have gotten a man from the LORD"* (Gen. 4:1). By Eve using the title *"LORD,"* which means "covenant God," and which refers to the *"seed"* of the woman (Gen. 3:15), she thought Cain was the promised one. She evidently didn't realize that it was impossible for fallen man to bring forth the promised Redeemer.

THE TRUE NATURE OF ISHMAEL

At any rate, the true nature of Ishmael was not revealed until the birth of Isaac. When Isaac came along, who was totally a work of the Holy Spirit, this began to glaringly reveal the true nature of Ishmael, whose true nature was that of murder (Gal. 4:29). That's the reason that the Lord told Sarah to tell Abraham that the bondwoman and her son had to go (Gal. 4:30-31).

In 1997, if I remember the time correctly, the Lord gave this evangelist the great revelation of the Cross. It was nothing new but actually that which had already been given to the Apostle Paul; however, it was that which the modern church did not know or understand. Beginning in 2011, this message began to be assimilated all over the world. The Lord gave us the platform by television to do that. In fact, at this particular time, we are now airing in some 90 million homes in America and more than 300 million in foreign countries. Coupling it all together, some 2 billion people can tune in to SonLife Broadcasting if they so desire.

The Message of the Cross being preached, taught, and proclaimed began to reveal what Ishmael actually was. In other words, all of the so-called schemes, manners, and ways of preachers, or whomever, claiming a victorious life were exposed for what they were, concoctions of men and not the Lord. The command now is the same as then: The bondwoman and her son must go. In other words, there is no righteousness outside of the Cross, and that we must understand. We either give up Ishmael, or else Ishmael will destroy what semblance of the

Spirit of God that remains. In other words, one cannot have both. One or the other must go.

Thank God, even though it cost him dearly, Abraham did exactly what the Lord told him to do.

THE COST

Please understand that it will always and without fail cost the believer something to give up Ishmael. This is something in which he has placed his faith, his reputation, his money, his efforts, and his ability. He has loaded it up with Scriptures and made himself believe it is right. Whatever it is, if it's not the Cross, we must understand, and understand completely, that it simply won't work. It's not God's way. Now that the Message of the Cross, by the Holy Spirit, has made its debut, there remains no more excuse for a false direction. It is either righteousness or self-righteousness. Anything other than the Cross of Christ and our faith in that finished work will, without fail, bring about self-righteousness.

FILLED

One can be *filled* with the righteousness of God but only in one way. That is by making void all the efforts of righteousness by our own schemes, manners, and ways and, thereby, placing our faith exclusively in Christ and the Cross. Then the Holy Spirit has said that we would be filled with the righteousness of God. There is no other way.

THE MERCIFUL

"Blessed are the merciful: for they shall obtain mercy" (Mat. 5:7).

If one is to notice, there is a progression about these beatitudes. Incidentally, the word *beatitudes* literally means "blissful blessings."

The absolute beginning requirement is to be *"poor in spirit,"* which will result in a *"mourning,"* which, in this case, means that one feels bad when one remembers one's moral and spiritual poverty. This will result in one being *"meek,"* as should be obvious, which will bring about a *"hunger and thirst after righteousness."*

As a further result, properly knowing and realizing his own poverty of self-worthiness and realizing that the righteousness he possesses is given solely by the grace of God, this individual is quick to show mercy to others.

However, the word *mercy,* as it is expressed in "being merciful," portrays far more than just a feeling of pity. Instead, it shows itself in action that goes beyond the thought.

The idea is that as God has shown so much mercy to the individual, he in turn (the individual) will be quick to show mercy to others. Even though the phrase, *"For they shall obtain,"* is in the positive sense, still, it has a tremendous negative sense in it as well.

FAILURE TO SHOW MERCY

The idea is that if one does not show mercy to others, and this means in action as well as thought, God will not show mercy to us. Realizing how dependent we are on the mercy of God, we should be quick to obey.

The type of mercy of which God is speaking is that which He shows to those who are poor in spirit. It is the mercy that is shown to those who hunger and thirst after righteousness with no way to obtain such themselves and, as well, no fit receptacle for God's righteousness. Yet He shows mercy and gives the righteousness anyway simply because we realize our destitute condition and hungrily desire Him to change it, even though we in no way are worthy of such. He then shows mercy and gives us what we need. We are to do the same to others; however, what does that mean?

THE RIGHTFUL WAY OF MERCY

As the previous verses speak of the poverty of soul and God's mercy granted despite such, it, as well, speaks of the believer who does not condemn because he has no right to condemn.

This is that of which Paul was speaking when he said, *"Brethren, if a man be overtaken in a fault* (a moral fault), *you who are spiritual, restore such an one in the spirit of meekness; considering yourself, lest you also be tempted."*

He then said, *"Bear you one another's burdens,"* which means to sympathize, show mercy and love, and not browbeat a fallen brother. He said this would *"fulfill the law of Christ,"* which, no doubt, spoke of this beatitude.

He then went on to say, *"For if a man think himself to be something, when he is nothing, he deceives himself"* (Gal. 6:1-3).

This means that if he puts himself above the one with the fault, he is only deceiving himself (Gal. 6:1-3).

THE BIBLICAL MEANING OF MERCY

Sometime in eternity past, God made a choice as to how He would deal with fallen man. This was before the foundation of the world and, of course, before man was created (I Pet. 1:18-20). Through foreknowledge, knowing that man would fall, God made a choice that He would deal with man by the means of grace. Grace has to be a choice or it isn't grace, which we will explain more in a moment. However, once grace was chosen as the means, God had no choice but to show mercy.

Now, we must understand that grace is not an automatic thing. In fact, it is the Cross of Christ that makes the grace of God possible. Without the Cross, there would be no grace because there could be no grace. Even before the Cross, the sacrificial system, which began on the first page of human history (Gen., Chpt. 4), made it possible for God to show grace, even though in a limited way. It means that man is not worthy of anything that God gives us and could not be worthy of such. However, if man will only express faith in the Cross of Christ, God will always grant His grace, which will always and without exception be followed by mercy. It must be remembered that the Cross of Christ is what makes everything possible. In other words, if there is no Cross, there is no grace and no mercy.

THE PURE IN HEART

"Blessed are the pure in heart: for they shall see God" (Mat. 5:8).

The *"pure in heart"* speaks of those who have received a new moral nature in regeneration. It is not man's standard of purity but God's, which is of far greater magnitude than man could ever begin to think.

There is only One who has been truly pure in heart, and that is Christ. All of the above, as expressed in the previous beatitudes, have not purity of heart, at least within themselves. However, they realize such and, therefore, the purity of Christ is freely given unto them. Consequently, they have purity that far exceeds any standard of man.

Regrettably, man, and even most of the church, will not accept God's freely given purity of heart, which can be brought about in a very short period of time. Conversely, God will not accept man's standard of purity.

Man's standard consists of religious rules and regulations, which deal altogether with the externals. God's purity deals with the heart, which is the seat of one's passions and emotions, which then expresses itself in the externals.

To sum up, no matter how sincere, man, within his own ability, strength, talent, and efforts, cannot make himself pure. There's only one thing that can do that, and that is one's faith expressed totally and completely in Christ and what Christ has done for us at the Cross. Then an unadulterated purity is granted to such an individual. If man looks to himself, he will be sorely disappointed. If he looks to Christ and what Christ did at the

Cross and, thereby, places his faith, instant purity will be his (Rom. 6:1-14; 8:1-11; I Cor. 1:17-18, 23; 2:2; Col. 2:10-15).

FOR THEY SHALL SEE GOD

The phrase, *"For they shall see God,"* is a beautiful and wonderful promise!

Seeing God does not speak of seeing Him with the physical eyes, but instead, seeing Him manifested in one's life. In other words, they will cease to see their own efforts in trying to make themselves pure, but will rather see that which God brings about, which will be glorious and wonderful indeed!

Consequently, the progression continues as it ascends from poverty of spirit to pureness of heart.

To see God work in one's life is the most wonderful, the greatest, and the most fulfilling thing that could ever be. Until one has sensed the presence of God, one does not really know what life is. Serving the Lord is the most rewarding enterprise, the most fulfilling of one's efforts, the greatest giver of peace and joy, and the most wonderful life and living in which one could ever begin to engage. Then, one is truly seeing God.

THE PEACEMAKERS

"Blessed are the peacemakers: for they shall be called the children of God" (Mat. 5:9).

The idea of this beatitude is not so much the individual attempting to make peace between warring factions in the military, the material, or the physical sense, as it is the proclaiming of God's way as expressed in these beatitudes, which brings peace to the troubled soul.

The self-righteous man, whether believer or otherwise, has no peace within his heart because he has no peace with God. Self-righteousness just might be the worst sin there is because in its pride, it is so deceptive.

This sin of self-ability or self-righteousness resulted from the fall and characterizes the war that constantly rages between God and man.

This self-righteousness flows over into our will power. While the will of man is most definitely important—*"whosoever will let him take of the water of life freely"*—still, man cannot live for God by that method. The believer's answer is faith; however, it must be faith in Christ and what Christ has done for us at the Cross.

Making the Cross of Christ the object of our faith, and maintaining it as the object of our faith, is what is demanded of the believer (I Cor. 1:17-18, 23; 2:2).

With our faith properly placed and maintained, the Holy Spirit, who works entirely within the parameters of the finished work of Christ, will then mightily help the believer. The Cross of Christ is the key (Rom. 8:1-11).

THE CROSS OF CHRIST
AND SELF-RIGHTEOUSNESS

Any direction taken by the believer, and I mean any direction other than the Cross of Christ, always and without exception concludes in self-righteousness. The church has no understanding whatsoever regarding the Cross and our sanctification because the Cross of Christ has been so little preached in the last several decades, and maybe even longer than that. This means that the modern church is the most self-righteous that it has been since the Reformation.

With self-righteousness, there is always a seething anger right beneath the surface, and we are speaking of believers now. In other words, the person stays angry most all the time and really doesn't know the reason. This is something that medical science cannot correct, etc.

MAN'S FOOLISH WAYS

Now, please read the following very carefully:

Reading out of a particular so-called study Bible the other day, one of our panel members on our daily telecast, *The Message Of The Cross*, read for us and the audience the recommendation given by the one who wrote the notes in that particular Bible as to how to overcome temptation.

His solution was that the individual under attack by Satan do 25 to 50 push-ups. If that wasn't enough, then do 25 to 50 sit-ups. Now, that was supposed to overcome temptation.

How ludicrous can we be? How ridiculous can we be? How absolutely absurd can we be?

I'm afraid that the believer is up against far more in the spirit world of darkness than the foolishness just described, but that's about all the modern church presently knows.

GOD'S PRESCRIBED ORDER OF VICTORY

As we have previously stated in this volume, due to its vast significance, we will say it again.

The following is the answer, and it doesn't really matter too much what the problem is:

- Jesus Christ is the source of all things we receive from God (Jn. 1:1-3, 14, 29; 14:6; Col. 2:10-15).

- Jesus Christ is the source, and the Cross of Christ is the means, and the only means, by which all of these great things are given to us (Rom. 6:1-14; I Cor. 1:17-18, 23; 2:2).

- With Jesus Christ being the source and the Cross being the means, this means that the Cross of Christ must ever be the object of our faith (Gal., Chpt. 5; 6:14; Col. 2:10-15).

- Christ is the source and the Cross is the means and, as well, the object of our faith. The Holy Spirit is God, who can do anything, and who works exclusively within the parameters of the finished work of Christ, i.e., the Cross. Therefore, the Holy Spirit will then work mightily within our hearts and lives to make us what we ought to be, without which, it simply cannot be done (Rom. 8:1-11; Eph. 2:13-18).

Now, biblically, this is God's solution for the human race, and it is His only solution because no other is needed. If the believer will do what we are saying, he will find that ultimately, sin will no longer have dominion over him. While the Bible does not teach sinless perfection, it most definitely does teach that sin is not to have dominion over us (Rom. 6:14). The only way this can be brought about is by faith in Christ and what He has done for us at the Cross.

This which we have described, to be sure, brings peace to the troubled soul.

THE CHILDREN OF GOD

As a child of God, we have many prerogatives; however, we will find as we search that all of these prerogatives are found in the Cross of Christ. In fact, the entirety of the story of the Bible, all the way from Genesis 1:1 through Revelation 22:21, is the story, in one way or the other, of Jesus Christ and Him crucified. In fact, every lamb offered in Old Testament times by the people of God was a type of Christ and the sacrifice of Himself on the Cross. When we look at it in that light, then it becomes very obvious as to the biblical portrayal as it regards the Cross of Christ.

So, when our faith is in Christ and the Cross, our faith is in the Word of God because that's what the Word of God actually teaches. In very abbreviated form, I have just given you God's prescribed order of victory, that for which our Lord paid such a price. To be sure, considering the price that He paid, it doesn't sit too very well with Him when we strike out on our own, trying to do what we cannot do. This means that we are ignoring the Lord, which means, in effect, that we are actually insulting Him. I'll say it again: I don't think the Lord is too very pleased with that!

PERSECUTION

"Blessed are they who are persecuted for righteousness' sake: for theirs is the kingdom of heaven" (Mat. 5:10).

If the believer doesn't know and understand the Cross of Christ relative to sanctification—how we live for God, how we order our behavior, how we have victory over the world, the flesh, and the Devil, and how we grow in grace and the knowledge of the Lord—and, thereby, places his faith in something else, Satan can definitely override the will of such a person and force him into a course of action that he does not desire to embrace (Rom. 7:18).

Some may think that if the believer is forced against his will, then he is not responsible. That is incorrect! He is responsible in that he has rejected God's way, which is the Cross, whether through ignorance or otherwise. At any rate, the results are the same.

As stated, while willpower is definitely important, within itself, it is not enough. We must exercise our faith in Christ and what Christ has done for us at the Cross. Then, as also stated, the Holy Spirit, who works exclusively within the parameters of the finished work of Christ, will work mightily on our behalf.

PERSECUTION

The phrase, *"Blessed are they who are persecuted for righteousness' sake,"* means that those who operate from the realm of self-righteousness will persecute those who trust in God's righteousness. This is a persecution that will come without fail! This is the war that began even in the garden of Eden.

An excellent example is Abraham, Isaac, and Ishmael.

Ishmael was a work of the flesh, the product of the scheming and planning of Sarah and Abraham. This means that God didn't have anything to do with it and, in fact, was greatly opposed to such action.

At any rate, Ishmael's true nature, which was a work of the flesh, was not exposed at all until the birth of Isaac, who was a work of the Spirit. That's when the problem began. In fact, Ishmael tried to kill Isaac and if he had been allowed to remain, he would have done so. This tells us that the Spirit and the flesh cannot coincide. One or the other must go.

The Lord told Sarah to tell Abraham that the bondwoman and her son must go (Gal. 4:30).

However, the point is, the true nature of Ishmael was not revealed or exposed until the advent of Isaac.

THE MESSAGE OF THE CROSS

Likewise, the schemes of religious man, such as we have just given concerning the push-ups, the sit-ups, etc., had not been exposed as to what all of that really is (which is a work of the flesh) until the Message of the Cross made its debut. As we have begun to preach this message, which has gone out and is going out all over the world, it is exposing the foolishness that abounds in modern Christendom as it regards means and ways of living for God.

With the advent of the Message of the Cross, which is of the Spirit because it is of the Word, all of this other stuff has been and is being exposed. Please understand that as Abraham did not want to give up Ishmael, even though he did, the modern church does not want to give up its Ishmaels either. To be sure, Ishmael will most definitely persecute Isaac exactly as our Lord said would happen.

THE KINGDOM OF HEAVEN

The phrase, *"For theirs is the kingdom of heaven,"* proclaims the fact that it is only the *righteousness of God* that will make it, so to speak. Self-righteousness won't work! Because it is so important, let us say it again:

If our faith is placed in anything other than Christ and the Cross, self-righteousness is the inevitable result.

YOU ARE BLESSED

"Blessed are you, when men shall revile you, and persecute you, and shall say all manner of evil against you falsely, for My sake" (Mat. 5:11).

It's a strange statement, "You are blessed!"

Jesus said that when men revile us, persecute us, and say all manner of evil against us falsely for His sake, then we are blessed. This means several things.

- It means that if the world pats you on the back, something is wrong with you!

- It means that if the world applauds what you are and what you are doing, whatever it is, it's not the gospel of Jesus Christ.

- It comes down to the fact that there is an offense to the Cross (Gal. 5:11).

We must understand that all victory is found totally and completely in the Cross of Christ. In fact, it is impossible for any believer to live a holy life without understanding the Cross of Christ relative not only to salvation but, as well, to sanctification.

Virtually all of Paul's writings in his 14 epistles deal with our living for God. Paul preached the Cross!

WHAT IS THE OFFENSE OF THE CROSS?

Perhaps we should first of all ask the question as to *why is there an offense to the Cross.*

It would seem that it couldn't be possible for the Cross of Christ to be an offense to anyone, but yet, it is. The Holy Spirit through Paul said it is (Gal. 5:11).

Why?

The Cross of Christ is God's only way—and we mean the only way for the sinner to be saved and the only way for the saint to be sanctified. When the Message of the Cross begins to be proclaimed, it exposes all the schemes of man, and we speak especially of religious man. The Message of the Cross was given to the Apostle Paul, which means it's by no means new. In Paul's day, it was the law of Moses that was used by many to oppose the Cross, and more specifically, it centered up in circumcision.

It is something else now, but it really doesn't matter what it is, or what it means. When preachers, or any believer for that matter, put their hope, their money, their reputation, or their belief system in the schemes devised by themselves or other men and are then told that they are wasting their time or that it won't work, such doesn't sit too very well. That is where the offense is. It lays waste and lays bare all of the foolishness of men. So, they strike out at the one preaching the Message of the Cross.

THE WORD OF GOD

To my recollection, I haven't had a single person scripturally try to repudiate our message as it regards the Cross of Christ. Of course, the reason is very simple. They don't do such because they cannot scripturally do such. To be sure, they are quick to attack me personally, and to do so vehemently. However, to attack the message, I haven't noticed that, at least up to this time.

The Cross of Christ is the very centerpiece of the Word of God. In fact, the Cross is such a part of Christianity, actually the bedrock of Christianity, that when it is mentioned, it is automatically known as to what it is. It is the gospel (I Cor. 1:17)!

Let me give you another example of some of the foolishness being promoted as the answer to the sin problem.

MORE FOOLISH DIRECTIONS

A pastor, with whom I was not acquainted, wrote me the other day, telling me how that he had found the answer to the sin problem. He was invited to a symposium with only preachers present. It must be understood that these were preachers who were supposed to be Spirit-filled but most definitely, as I think was proven, were not Spirit-led. At any rate, I am somewhat acquainted with the leader of all of this, who is, in fact, one of the leaders in one of the major Pentecostal denominations.

All of the preachers and their wives were told to bring a pad and pencil with them to this meeting. The moderator spoke for quite some time and then told them to do the following:

- They were to write all of their sins down on the pad that they had brought with them.

- Then each one was to select a mate other than his or her husband or wife, in other words, a man to a man and a woman to a woman, and to stand facing each other.

- They were to then read out loud to each other the sins they had written down. The man who wrote me was quick to state that his sins were not nearly as bad as some of the others.

- After they read out all of these sins, then they were to tear the paper from the pad and rip it into little pieces.

- They were then to drop the pieces on the floor and jump up and down on them, while shouting the praises of the Lord. This was supposed to bring victory.

THE CROSS

I wrote him back without really explaining anything and said to him, "My brother, the only answer for sin is the Cross of Christ." As stated, I didn't bother to explain it because I could tell from his letter that it would not have done any good. The modern church is constantly coming up with foolishness such as this, which must anger the Lord greatly. Let us say it again: The only answer for sin is the Cross of Christ. Exactly as our Lord said, when we place our faith and trust exclusively in Christ and the Cross, which means to repudiate all of this foolishness, it's not going to sit well, and there's going to be some persecution (Heb. 10:12, 18).

REWARD

"Rejoice, and be exceeding glad: for great is your reward in heaven: for so persecuted they the prophets which were before you" (Mat. 5:12).

When we are persecuted for our stand for Christ, we are to *"rejoice, and be exceeding glad."* With that being the case, we are told that great is our reward in heaven. We must understand that we are not the first to undergo such, for the prophets were persecuted before us.

SALT OF THE EARTH

"You are the salt of the earth: but if the salt have lost his savor, wherewith shall it be salted? it is thenceforth good for nothing, but to be cast out, and to be trodden under foot of men" (Mat. 5:13).

The phrase, *"You are the salt of the earth,"* is meant to portray the believer as *"salt"* in the world, with salt serving as a symbol of a preservative.

Therefore, the Lord is saying that only those who fall into the category of the Beatitudes really constitute a deterrent to evil and a preservative of righteousness.

At the same time, He is saying that all of man's self efforts at improvement only add to the problem instead of solving it.

In fact, it is the Cross of Christ alone and our faith in that finished work that gives the Holy Spirit latitude to work within our lives, which will bring about the desired result.

If the preacher doesn't preach the Cross, whatever it is he is preaching might be good, and it might be partly gospel, but it is only the Cross that proclaims the total gospel.

Paul said to preach the Cross (I Cor. 1:23).

It must be understood that there is no such thing as moral evolution. In other words, if one does certain things regarding motivation, etc., the champion within him will ultimately be brought out. Nothing could be further from the truth.

THE LOST PRESERVATIVE

The question, *"But if the salt have lost his savor, wherewith shall it be salted?"* refers to the fact that if the salt loses its preservative power, there is nothing to take its place! It is the one and only property that will prevent corruption.

The Christian's one mission in life is to guard the church from corruption by conduct and doctrine. That is the reason Jude said, *"That you should earnestly contend for the faith which was once delivered unto the saints."*

Jude further said, *"For there are certain men crept in unawares, who were before of old ordained to this condemnation, ungodly men, turning the grace of our God into lasciviousness, and denying the only Lord God, and our Lord Jesus Christ"* (Jude, Vss. 3-4).

HOW DOES A CHRISTIAN LOSE HIS SAVOR?

The Christian who doesn't understand the Cross as it regards our sanctification, in other words, how we live for God, is a person, although saved, who really has no preservative. The Christian who has heard the Message of the Cross and has rejected it has placed himself in a position to where he is no longer of worth to the kingdom of God. It is only through the Cross of Christ that the believer can be what he or she ought to be. Anything else is a waste. It is the Cross and the Cross alone.

I'm certain that the reader understands that when we speak of the Cross, we aren't speaking of the wooden beam on which Jesus died, but rather what He there accomplished.

What did He accomplish on the Cross?

First of all, He atoned for all sin—past, present, and future —at least for all who will believe. That within itself is of such magnitude as to defy all description. However, considering that sin is the means by which Satan steals, kills, and destroys, this means that Satan, every fallen angel, and every demon spirit also were totally and completely defeated. Paul said concerning this: *"Blotting out the handwriting of ordinances that was against us, which was contrary to us, and took it out of the way, nailing it to His Cross; And having spoiled principalities and powers, He made a show of them openly, triumphing over them in it"* (Col. 2:14-15).

The word *triumphing* means that Christ totally defeated all of these powers of darkness and did so on our behalf. I remind the reader that it was all done at the Cross.

WHAT IS THE GOSPEL OF JESUS CHRIST?

Paul tells us exactly what it is. He said, *"Christ sent me not to baptize, but to preach the gospel: not with wisdom of words, lest the Cross of Christ should be made of none effect"* (I Cor. 1:17). In this short passage, he tells us exactly what the gospel is. It is the *"Cross of Christ."*

Let us say it this way: Jesus Christ is the new covenant. That does not mean that He has the new covenant or has perfected the new covenant, but that He is the new covenant. The meaning of the new covenant is the Cross of Christ, the meaning of which was given to the apostle Paul, which the great apostle gave to us in his 14 epistles. In fact, one might say and be totally correct that the story of the Bible from cover to cover is *"Jesus Christ and Him crucified."*

It began before the universe was ever created, which, of course, was before man was ever created. Through foreknowledge, the Godhead knew that man would fall, and it was determined that man would be redeemed by God becoming man and, thereby, going to the Cross in order to redeem the fallen sons of Adam's lost race (I Pet. 1:18-20).

After the fall of man, it was determined on the first page of human history that the Cross was the foundation of all that God would do. We find that in Chapter 4 of Genesis as it regards the illustration of Cain and Abel. After that, millions of lambs were offered, at least until Christ came. All were symbols of the Son of the living God, who would give Himself as a sacrifice on the Cross of Calvary.

Upon the fall of man, the Lord introduced the sacrificial system to the fallen first family. If carried out according to His instructions, it would bring about forgiveness of sins and would allow Adam and Eve and all who would follow to have communion and fellowship with Him. That lasted for nearly 4,000 years until the Cross itself. As everything looked toward the Cross then, everything looks back to the Cross now. Then, it was the prophetic Jesus, while now, it is the historic Jesus.

So, if the *"preaching of the Cross"* is, in fact, the gospel, that means that the modern church has totally and completely lost its savor. The truth is, the Cross of Christ, which is the gospel, is precious little preached anymore. It is preached in some circles for salvation, and thank God for that, but almost not at all for sanctification. In virtually all of Paul's writings (who gave us this great truth), he dwells on how we live for God, in other words, our sanctification.

THE SONLIFE BROADCASTING NETWORK

While I've been on television longer than any other preacher in the world, except one other, still, all of our broadcast time was a program that was one hour a week and 30 minutes a day. However, in 2010, we went on—because the Lord told us to do so—24 hours a day, seven days a week. At this time, we are in some 90 million homes in America and over 300 million in foreign countries. We are going through every door that the Lord opens. This is what we believe that He has called us to do. The Message of the Cross must be given to the entirety of the world, and especially the church. Considering that the Cross of Christ alone stands between mankind and the judgment of God (and to be sure, that is true), then the possibility definitely exists that this Message of the Cross could very well hold back the judgment of God on this nation and even the world, at least for a period of time.

GOOD FOR NOTHING

Jesus said, "*It is thenceforth good for nothing, but to be cast out, and to be trodden under foot of men.*" (Mat. 5:13).

This means that most of the so-called modern gospel is of no value whatsoever. As one of my dear preacher friends, who is now with the Lord, said, "Those churches should be turned into grocery stores." He went on to say, "They would help the public much more than what they are presently doing." How true that is!

There is only one answer for the entire situation, and that is to come back to the Cross. I say that, and yet, most churches, I fear, have never been to the Cross in the first place. God help us!

THE LIGHT OF THE WORLD

"You are the light of the world. A city that is set on an hill cannot be hid" (Mat. 5:14).

The statement, *"You are the light of the world,"* is powerful indeed. This means that the believer is not only light, but in fact, the *only* light. However, this is light that is derived solely from Christ, hence, Him saying in verse 11, *"For My sake."*

As Christ graphically brought out in the Beatitudes, the believer, within himself, has no light as he has no salvation; consequently, all must be drawn from Christ. He alone is that Light, with those who make Him Lord of their lives becoming reflectors of that Light. This means that the so-called great universities of the world provide no light, except that which is derived from the Word of God, whether advertently or inadvertently.

This (the light) is the reason that the Christlike child of God is of such value and consequence wherever he may be. However, such worth will not at all be recognized by the world, and seldom by the church.

The phrase, *"A city that is set on an hill cannot be hid,"* simply means that as such a city is obvious to all, likewise, the Christian should have light that is obvious to all.

THE HIDDEN LIGHT

"Neither do men light a candle, and put it under a bushel, but on a candlestick; and it gives light unto all who are in the house" (Mat. 5:15).

The idea of this verse concerns the purpose of the true believer in this world.

The phrase, *"Neither do men light a candle, and put it under a bushel,"* really speaks of asceticism, which refers to an individual who shuts himself away as a hermit.

Jesus is saying that if His followers who are truly endowed with His righteousness and, therefore, His light, hide themselves away as some have advocated, their very purpose, at least as far as the world is concerned, will be lost. Consequently, it is not God's intention that His people bunch up in little communities, as some have tried, in order to build a paradise, which, incidentally, has always failed. Instead, we are to live in the very midst of society as salt and light and, therefore, to be a restraining influence against evil.

THE CANDLESTICK

The phrase, *"But on a candlestick; and it gives light unto all who are in the house,"* is meant to proclaim, as is obvious, the place where our Lord wants His children, which is where they can give light in the midst of the darkness.

So, if you are the only believer in the midst of a group of unbelievers at your daily employment, etc., do not lament the fact, but instead, thank the Lord that He has put you in a place of darkness where your light can shine. It is designed thusly by the Lord.

A PERSONAL EXPERIENCE

Years ago when Frances and I first married, and I was just beginning in the ministry, I secured a job with a plumbing contractor. It was not a large operation, with only about eight or 10 employees, of which I was one.

The man who owned the company was one of the vilest, most profane, and most wicked men that I had personally known. It seemed as if every word out of his mouth was profanity. The men who worked with him, with some of them professing to know the Lord, were little better than he, if at all.

After a very short time, they knew of my devotion to Christ, with him exclaiming with a sardonic laugh that in just a few days, I would be exactly like them—telling dirty jokes, cursing, etc.

By the grace of God, the very opposite happened. Little by little, those men began to ask me questions about the Bible, which often took the place of their profane conversation of the past.

I was even able to get some of them in church with me, at least for a time or two, even though to my knowledge, none of them truly accepted the Lord.

However, I was unable whatsoever to get the owner of the company to church or anything that looked like church.

I only worked there about six months, if that, and then left for other endeavors.

THE CONVICTING POWER
OF THE HOLY SPIRIT

Many years passed, with our ministry growing, until our telecast at a given point in time covered a sizeable part of the earth.

It was in the early part of 1987, if I remember correctly, that I received a letter from the daughter of the contractor for whom I had worked so long ago—the one, incidentally, who was so profane. She told me how that her dad was faithfully watching the telecast and had made the statement, "If I ever get it, I want what Jimmy Swaggart has," speaking of those days when I worked with him those many years before.

A few months later, I received another letter from her, telling me that her dad had passed away. Then she added, "Brother Swaggart, just before he died, he prayed the sinner's prayer with you as he was watching the telecast and truly gave his heart and life to Jesus Christ."

When I read the letter, I could not help but weep for joy. I didn't think that *light* had shown so brightly, but it had!

In fact, no true light of the gospel is wasted. It always garners its intended results, even though it may take time to do so.

THE MORAL CHARACTERISTICS

"Let your light so shine before men, that they may see your good works, and glorify your Father who is in heaven" (Mat. 5:16).

As we have briefly alluded, verses 3 through 16 set out the moral characteristics of the citizens of the kingdom of the heavens, and so it is apparent that the new birth is an absolute necessity for entrance into that kingdom.

The idea of this verse is a continuance of the previous. The Lord lays stress on personal possession of light, personal action, personal relationship, and origin.

In other words, the light should produce good works, which will be seen by men, but is not necessarily done just for that purpose. Rather, it is to carry out the commandment of the Lord, which will glorify God.

THE ROMAN EMPIRE

Christianity made inroads into the mighty Roman Empire because of this very thing. The morality of Christianity was so much higher than that espoused by Rome, which gradually won many over.

It will do and, in fact, does the same presently!

However, this is not to be confused with the effort of the modern Christendom to "Christianize society." The two are completely different!

One attempts to serve as a light, which will glorify God and show men the way. The other seeks to change society by political means, which, in fact, cannot be done, as the tenor of these verses brings out. The true believer is, as stated, salt and light, which has great reference to making things greater, for which they are intended. However, the whole of society will not and, in fact, cannot be changed until the second coming of Christ.

DOMINIONISM

This light and the producing of good works have no relationship to the modern teaching of dominionism, which teaches that Christianity will ultimately overcome all other religions, finally become supreme, and will then beckon Christ to come back. Nothing could be so prideful and so unscriptural as that ridiculous doctrine. The Bible teaches the very opposite.

In these last days, things are not going to get better and better as these people teach, but rather worse and worse (I Tim. 4:1; II Tim. 3:1-5; 4:3-4).

Neither is the church to be reduced to the place of mere service, thinking that such works are the mission of the church. They aren't!

The mission of the church is to preach the gospel of Jesus Christ and Him crucified to the entirety of the world. Man is lost, and there is only one thing that will save him, and that isn't good works as we think of such. The type of good works that the Word of God brings out has to do with the proclamation of the gospel, which changes lives. Then drunkards are made sober, prostitutes are made pure, harlots are made holy, and thieves are made honest. In fact, the list goes on and on, which the gospel alone can do. Those are the good works of which the Holy Spirit here speaks.

THE GOSPEL

If we look at the book of Acts and the Epistles in the New Testament, what do we see? We see preachers proclaiming the gospel, healing the sick, and believing God to touch hearts and lives, which changes lives and changes entire communities. Those are the *"good works"* of which the Lord here speaks, not some glorified religious peace corps.

As we have previously stated, the true believer is salt and light, which has great reference to making things better, for which they are intended. In fact, every iota of freedom and prosperity in this world is because of the Word of God and the millions of people who are truly born again. You lose that and you lose your prosperity, and you lose your freedom, which is exactly what is presently happening in America.

In his inaugural address, President Obama stated that America is not Christian but is a mix of Christian, Islam, atheist, etc. He is the only president to ever make such a statement, with all others referring to the fact that America is a Christian nation, meaning that the predominant belief system is Christianity, i.e., the Bible. President Obama could not be more wrong. This nation is not Islamic, and God help us if we ever get to be even partially Islamic. In fact, the religion of Islam is the most demonic religion ever spawned by hell itself, and to be sure, that's exactly where it was conceived and birthed.

ISLAM

Mrs. Hillary Rodham Clinton, the former secretary of state of this nation, made the statement sometime back, and I paraphrase, that "sharia law is not so bad." I wonder if Mrs. Clinton even remotely understands what she is saying. I think not!

Sharia law states that if a Muslim converts to Christianity, he is to be instantly executed. If a daughter in a Muslim family is raped, they do nothing with the man, but they kill the girl. Now, that's a nice religion, isn't it? In fact, according to sharia law, women in the religion of Islam are treated as cheap goods. If somebody steals something, they chop off his hands. Is that what our distinguished Mrs. Clinton desires? As well, she should understand that the Koran teaches that everyone in the world must be converted to Islam, or else, they will be made slaves or executed. To be sure, if Islam had its way, in other words, if they had the power, they would demand what I've just stated—convert to Islam, or be killed or made a slave.

While all Muslims aren't murderers, the truth is, all Muslims, at least if they are true to the Koran, are in sympathy with the murderers.

THE RELIGION

We spent more than a trillion dollars in Iraq and suffered the loss of more than 4,000 young men and young ladies in battle, besides the thousands wounded, and the moment we left, it reverted right back to what it was, or worse. The same thing will happen in Afghanistan. What our leaders refuse to realize or believe is that they are up against a religion. Our leaders thought they could democratize these countries, but they can't. There's something else we had best understand: While we aren't at war with the religion of Islam, the religion of Islam is most definitely at war with us. They hate us. They call Israel the Little Satan and America the Great Satan.

These people live by the Koran, and please understand, that book, despite what former President Bush said, is not a book of peace, but the very opposite. Again, despite what former President Bush said, Christians and Muslims do not pray to the same God. Allah, the so-called God of the Muslims, is actually a demon spirit. The name *Allah* was selected by Muhammad from a bevy of Babylonian names typifying their supposed gods. No sir, Mr. President, when we pray to our heavenly Father, the God of the Bible, our Creator and, as well, our Saviour, we are not praying to a demon spirit or a Babylonian entity as the Muslims, but rather the Lord of glory. Make no mistake about that!

MURDERERS?

As we have just stated, while all Muslims aren't murders, still, virtually all Muslims totally and completely agree with the murderers. In other words, they are in favor of anything the fanatics do in order to help destroy America. From the time the children in a Muslim home are able to comprehend anything, they are taught to hate America and to hate Israel.

Virtually every mosque in America is a place to foment plans of destruction for America.

The truth is, political correctness is killing us. The Trojan horse is not sneaking into this nation; it's coming in with open-faced declaration as to what they're going to do to this nation. We are so stupid that, sadly and regrettably, we are aiding and abetting that which they desire to do. It's no longer Uncle Sam, but it is rather Uncle Sap.

There is no light but Jesus Christ. He alone is the answer to dying humanity. He alone died on Calvary's Cross that we might be able to have and enjoy eternal life. Yet, I must say that the situation in this world is not going to change, but rather grow worse, much worse. The world is staring pell-mell at the coming great tribulation outlined in the book of Revelation. We can hide our heads in the sand and claim that it's not going to take place, but it is.

Yes, things are going to change and for the better, much better, far better, miraculously better, but only when Jesus Christ comes back, and come back He will!

THE LAW OF MOSES

"Think not that I am come to destroy the law, or the prophets: I am not come to destroy, but to fulfill" (Mat. 5:17).

This law, even though given to Moses, is actually the law of God. It is God's standard of righteousness built around, one might say, the Ten Commandments (Ex., Chpt. 20). In fact, every single fair and equitable law on the face of the earth presently, and that has ever been since the law of Moses was given, if traced back far enough, will always be traced back to the Ten Commandments.

Admittedly, there were laws in the world before the law of Moses; however, they were grossly unfair and weighted heavily toward the rich and the powerful, with the poor and helpless given little recourse at all. In fact, the law of Moses is the only fair, equitable, and impartial law that has ever been given. It addressed every facet of life and living among the Jews. It excluded nothing and included everything.

Under the new covenant, which has replaced the old, the Bible does not teach sinless perfection, but it most definitely does teach that sin is not to have dominion over the believer (Rom. 6:14).

The sad fact is that because believers do not understand the Cross of Christ relative to sanctification—how we live for God—sin is dominating most in some way.

God's plan of salvation and victory is the new covenant, to which the old covenant (the law of Moses) ever pointed, which is solely the Cross of Christ. Anytime we resist His plan of salvation and victory, we are resisting the Holy Spirit, which no sane person desires to do.

CHRIST

In a sense, the law of Moses proclaimed Christ in every aspect of its doing. Actually, in writing the book of Hebrews, the apostle Paul chose the tabernacle with all of its accoutrements, which are included in the law, to portray the Lord Jesus Christ. In fact, every part and particle of the tabernacle and its furnishings, and I mean everything, pointed to Christ in some way regarding the atoning work, mediatorial work, and intercessory work.

WHY WAS THE LAW GIVEN?

It was given for any number of reasons. Some of them are:

- As stated, the law of Moses was God's standard of righteousness. It was what God demanded of the human family.

- The law of Moses, at least at that time, was a pattern for living. It gave direction in every capacity of life and living.

- The law of Moses was given, despite its simplicity, to show man that he could not keep the law, no matter how hard he tried. In fact, it was virtually impossible. The only one who ever kept the law and did it perfectly, not sinning even one time in word, thought, or deed, was the Lord Jesus Christ.

- The law, as someone has well said, was like a mirror in which man looked at himself, but which gave no power to change what he saw. What he saw was not a pretty picture.

- The law, as all law must, contained a bitter penalty for breaking its concepts. That penalty was death, which referred to separation from God and ultimately, eternal hell.

- Despite its demands, the law gave no power to man for the law to be kept. Consequently, it was impossible for man to live up to its precepts.

WHY DID GOD NOT GIVE MAN POWER TO KEEP THE LAW?

At the very core of the law was the sacrificial system. Actually, were it not for that system, Israel would have been totally and completely destroyed. While the sacrificial system did not take away sins, it most definitely covered sin and, thereby, gave man another chance, so to speak. As would be obvious, this system was at work 24 hours a day, seven days a week. It is believed that from the time the law was given to Moses on Mount Sinai, more than 1 billion lambs were slaughtered during the intervening 1,500 years to the time of Christ. In fact, in the Passion Week when Jesus died, which was Passover, Josephus, the great Jewish historian, stated that there were approximately 250,000 lambs offered during that one week. However, the blood of bulls and goats could not take away sins (Heb. 10:4). This means that all of the animal blood that was shed was only a stopgap measure, which was meant to serve until the Redeemer would come. In other words, every lamb that was offered was a type of Christ, hence, John the Baptist saying when he introduced Christ, *"Behold the Lamb of God, who takes away the sin of the world"* (Jn. 1:29).

Such a term had never been used in Jewish history or in any other history. As stated, the blood of bulls and goats could not take away sins, but Jesus, by the vicarious offering of Himself on the Cross of Calvary, would atone for all sin and, thereby, take all sin away, at least for all who would believe (Jn. 3:16). Not only would that sin be taken away for the Jews, or any other particular group, but they would be taken away for the entirety of the world, again for those who will believe (Jn. 3:16).

My hope is built on nothing less,
Than Jesus' blood and righteousness,
I dare not trust the sweetest frame,
But wholly lean on Jesus' name.

On Christ the solid rock I stand;
All other ground is sinking sand,
All other ground is sinking sand.

THE SERMON
on the
MOUNT

CHAPTER 2

THE FOUNDATION OF
THE NEW COVENANT

THE FOUNDATION OF THE NEW COVENANT

"THINK NOT THAT I am come to destroy the law, or the prophets: I am not come to destroy, but to fulfil. For verily I say unto you, Till heaven and earth pass, one jot or one tittle shall in no wise pass from the law, till all be fulfilled" (Mat. 5:17-18).

JESUS, THE FULFILLMENT OF THE LAW

When Jesus came as the second man and the last Adam, meaning that He was God manifest in the flesh, He never used His powers of deity. As someone has well said, "While He in the incarnation, God becoming man, laid aside the expression of His deity, He never for a moment lost the possession of His deity."

As previously stated, He kept the law in every respect, never failing even one single time. He did it all for you and for me. So, our acceptance of Him transfers us from the position of law-breaker, which warrants death, to the position of law keeper. This is all because of our faith in Christ and what He has done for us.

However, there remained the terrible problem of the broken law, of which all were guilty. To answer that, Jesus would have to go to the Cross and would have to give Himself as a sacrifice in the shedding of His life's blood, which God would and did accept. Jesus Christ was not assassinated and was not executed; He was rather sacrificed.

In fact, He came to be a sacrifice—a sacrifice on the Cross. The Cross of Christ is the very center and the very foundation of Christianity. Remove the Cross, and you have nothing left but a vapid philosophy, which will save no one, deliver no one, and help no one. As we have repeatedly stated, Jesus Christ was and is the source of all the great, good, and wonderful things that we receive from God; however, the Cross of Christ is the means, and the only means, by which these things are given to us. Without the Cross, God could not even look at us, much less forgive our sins and have communion with us.

THE CROSS OF CHRIST

When Jesus died on the Cross, He atoned for every sin—past, present, and future—at least for all who will believe. This removed Satan's legal right to hold man captive. So, if he holds anyone captive presently, it is simply because the individual does not avail himself or herself of the privileges that are afforded us at Calvary's Cross. Never forget what Jesus did at the Cross, which means He died for you and for me and made a way for our salvation that we might be eternally saved. However, the Cross of Christ also addresses itself to our sanctification, in other words, how we live for God on a daily basis, how we grow in grace and the knowledge of the Lord, and how we have victory over the world, the flesh, and the Devil. It is all by the means of the Cross. All of this means that the Cross of Christ must be the object of our faith, and must totally be the object of our faith, which then gives the Holy Spirit the latitude to work within our hearts and within our lives.

THE LAW WAS FINISHED IN CHRIST

Paul said, *"For Christ is the end of the law for righteousness* (Christ fulfilled the totality of the law) *to everyone who believes* (faith in Christ guarantees the righteousness, which the law had but could not give)*"* (Rom. 10:4) (The Expositor's Study Bible).

What does that mean?

That means the law of God is no more, at least for the believer, simply because it was totally fulfilled in Christ, and, as stated, it was done exclusively for us. That's why we say repeatedly that Jesus' death on the Cross was not an incident, an accident, an assassination, or an execution. It was a sacrifice. In fact, Jesus came to this world to go to the Cross. While He did many things, the Cross was ever in view and was ever meant to be His destination.

WHAT ABOUT THE TEN COMMANDMENTS?

They were fulfilled as well; however, because they are moral laws, they cannot change and are still in force. So, it is not that the Ten Commandments be kept, which we as believers know must be done, but it's how they are kept. In other words, how do we keep these commandments under the new covenant?

The *how* is totally in Christ.

The first thing that the Christian must realize is that we are not to live our lives by law. We are to live it by Christ, referring to faith in what He has done for us and is doing for us. If the believer will place his or her faith exclusively in Christ and what Christ has done for us at the Cross, understanding that it was at the Cross that all victory was won, then the Holy Spirit will work mightily within our hearts and lives. Then, the Ten Commandments, so to speak, will be kept, and kept perfectly, without our even giving it a thought. And yet, we must say that while nearly all the commandments were brought over into the new covenant, there is one that wasn't, which is the fourth, *"Remember the sabbath day to keep it holy"* (Ex. 20:8). Actually, that particular commandment is the only commandment that is not moral. So, what do we do about that commandment?

REMEMBER THE SABBATH TO KEEP IT HOLY

The fourth commandment about the Sabbath pertained to a day of rest, which was Saturday. It epitomized, symbolized, and portrayed the rest that one finds in Christ when our Lord is accepted as Saviour. That's what it symbolized. When Jesus came, all of that was fulfilled. In fact, the entire expression of the Sabbath pertained to the rest that one finds in Christ, that is, when one comes to Christ. It is the greatest thing in the world. Condemnation and guilt are lifted. There's a peace that passes all understanding because Jesus is that rest. That's what He was talking about when He said:

Come unto Me (is meant by Jesus to reveal Himself as the giver of salvation), *all you who labor and are heavy laden* (trying to earn salvation by works), *and I will give you rest* (this 'rest' can only be found by placing one's faith in Christ and what Christ has done for us at the Cross [Gal. 5:1-6]). *Take My yoke upon you* (the 'yoke' of the 'Cross' [Lk. 9:23]), *and learn of Me* (learn of His sacrifice [Rom. 6:3-5]); *for I am meek and lowly in heart* (the only thing that our Lord personally said of Himself): *and you shall find rest unto your souls* (the soul can find rest only in the Cross). *For My yoke is easy, and My burden is light* (what He requires of us is very little, just to have faith in Him and His sacrificial atoning work) (Mat. 11:28-30) (The Expositor's Study Bible).

When one accepts Christ, one then finds the rest that can only be found in Him.

It is rest from works of the law, from self-righteousness, from the terrible bondage of religion, etc. In fact, when a person accepts Christ, he is keeping the Sabbath, so to speak, not just one day of the week, but every day of the week, 24 hours a day, etc.

LAW OR GRACE

Romans 6:14 says, *"For sin shall not have dominion over you (us), for you (we) are not under the law, but under grace."*

This means that there are only two places that a human being can be—it is either *law* or *grace*. Sadly, because of the far greater majority of the modern church knowing almost nothing of the Cross of Christ respecting sanctification, most (and we speak of those who truly love the Lord) are living under law. It is a sad spectacle.

It guarantees failure because there is always a penalty to the law referred to as the *"curse"* (Gal. 3:10). It's a sad thing for believers presently to try to live under law in order to remove the penalty of the law, especially considering the price that our Lord paid at Calvary's Cross.

THE CROSS

In fact, the Word says concerning this very thing:

"Blotting out the handwriting of ordinances that was against us (pertains to the law of Moses, which was God's standard of righteousness that man could not reach), *which was contrary to us* (law is against us simply because we are unable to keep its precepts, no matter how hard we try), *and took it out of the way* (refers to the penalty of the law being removed), *nailing it to His Cross* (the law with its decrees was abolished in Christ's death as if crucified with Him" (Col. 2:14) (The Expositor's Study Bible).

Let us say it again: If the believer doesn't understand the Cross of Christ relative to our everyday living for God (Lk. 9:23), such a believer—no matter how much he loves God, no matter how sincere he is, and no matter how hard he tries—is instead going to live under law, which brings nothing but misery. As someone has well said, "Many people are truly saved, but they are miserably saved."

HOW DOES ONE LIVE UNDER GRACE?

That's the question!

Actually, it's very simple. Let's start out by defining grace.

Grace is simply the goodness of God given to undeserving people. Of course, that is an oversimplification, but who can properly explain grace? It is so broad, so wide, so gracious, and so wonderful that even the greatest theologians would not be able to fully explain the precepts of this great attribute called grace. However, let the reader understand that it is the Cross of Christ, and the Cross of Christ alone, and our faith in that finished work that makes grace available to us. It will not function in any other capacity but only tend to be frustrated (Gal. 2:21).

Let's say it again: Instead of trying to explain it fully and taking several pages to do so, I will simply say that every single blessing that we receive from the Lord constitutes the grace of God.

This means that we don't deserve it, but it's given to us anyway because of what Jesus did at the Cross and our faith in that vicarious work. The Cross of Christ opened up the way for God's grace to be given in an unlimited supply to any and all who will believe. Understand that. It is the Cross that makes the grace of God possible.

THE FINISHED WORK OF CHRIST

God had just as much grace in Old Testament times as He does now, but due to the fact that the blood of bulls and goats could not remove sins, He was limited as to what He could do as it regarded grace. But yet, even then, every soul that was saved or has ever been saved has always been saved strictly by the grace of God.

In fact, it can be no other way.

As we have previously stated, when the believer places his or her faith exclusively in Christ and what Christ has done for us at the Cross, the Holy Spirit, who is the dispenser of grace, will then work mightily on our behalf and help us to live this life that we ought to live.

However, we must understand that Jesus Christ is always the source, but the Cross is always the means by which all of these wonderful things come to us. We must maintain our faith in the Cross, otherwise, it's going to be law, and it won't be pleasant.

Please understand that just because this is the dispensation of grace, it doesn't mean that grace is automatic. If the believer places his faith in anything except the Cross, this frustrates the grace of God, which means that God cannot give to us what He desires to give.

The law was finished in Christ. He alone could finish this great precept. In fact, the law of God was always meant to be temporary, only until the great law keeper could come. Thank God, He has come.

WHAT DOES IT MEAN TO FRUSTRATE
THE GRACE OF GOD?

Paul said, *"I am crucified with Christ: nevertheless I live; yet not I, but Christ lives in me: and the life which I now live in the flesh I live by the faith of the Son of God, who loved me, and gave Himself for me. I do not frustrate the grace of God: for if righteousness come by the law, then Christ is dead in vain"* (Gal. 2:20-21).

Many Christians have the erroneous idea that due to the fact that we are living in the dispensation of grace, grace is just an automatic process. In other words, it is given automatically by God to the believer. Such is not correct. In fact, it is woefully incorrect.

When the believer places his or her faith in anything except Christ and the Cross, this frustrates the grace of God. The word *frustrate* in the Greek is "atheteo" and means "to set aside, to disesteem, to neutralize, to despise, to disannul, to bring to nought, to reject." So, the word *frustrate* chosen here by the Holy Spirit is strong indeed, but sadly, that's where most modern believers are. They are living in a state of frustration as it regards the grace of God. This means, as would be obvious, that they have stopped its process, meaning that this which God wants to give them cannot be given.

Even though we've already explained it, let's say it again: The way that one frustrates the grace of God is when faith is placed in anything except Christ and the Cross. It doesn't really matter what the other things are. They may be good things within their own right and totally scriptural if used scripturally. However, when used unscripturally, this seeks to frustrate the grace of God, which means to stop its flow.

For instance, when someone says that you can fast so many days, and all evil in your life will be defeated, or some such thought, this is wrong. Fasting is most definitely scriptural and will definitely bless the individual who partakes thereof, that is, if it's done correctly; however, fasting is not the way to overcome sin. It simply cannot be done that way. The only answer for sin (and to be sure, sin is the problem) is the Cross of Christ.

Paul said, *"So Christ was once offered to bear the sins of many"* (Heb. 9:28).

The apostle then said, *"But this man, after He had offered one sacrifice for sins forever, sat down on the right hand of God"* (Heb. 10:12).

Once again, let us say it: if faith is placed in anything other than Christ and the Cross, this automatically frustrates the grace of God, which places the believer in an extremely precarious position.

THE ULTIMATE AUTHORITY

"For verily I say unto you, Till heaven and earth pass, one jot or one tittle shall in no wise pass from the law, till all be fulfilled" (Mat. 5:18).

The Cross of Christ is the revealed truth of God's judgment on sin.

Never associate the idea of martyrdom with the Cross of Christ. It was the supreme triumph, and it shook the very foundations of hell.

Dietrich Bonhoeffer said, "There is nothing in time or eternity more absolutely certain and irrefutable than what Jesus Christ accomplished on the Cross."

The phrase, *"Verily I say unto you,"* proclaims the ultimate authority!

The scribes and the Pharisees seldom had a definitive answer, generally going into detail about things that had little to do with the question at hand.

Consequently, the people had very little qualitative leadership, if any.

TO BE CHANGED

The phrase, *"Till heaven and earth pass,"* does not mean that they will ultimately be destroyed. The Greek word for "pass" is *parerchomai* and means "to be changed or pass from one condition to another."

Actually, the heavens and the earth will never pass out of existence but will be changed and purified by fire, and thereby be renewed (Rom. 8:21-24; Heb. 1:10-12; 12:25-29; II Pet. 3:10-13; Rev. 21:1).

The Bible actually teaches that the heavens and the earth will remain forever (Ps. 72:17; 89:36-37; 104:5; Eccl. 1:4).

TILL ALL BE FULFILLED

The phrase, *"One jot or one tittle shall in no wise pass from the law,"* refers to the word *jot* as the smallest letter in the Hebrew alphabet, with the word *tittle* referring to the smallest ornament placed upon certain Hebrew letters.

The phrase, *"Till all be fulfilled,"* was brought to pass in Christ, who fulfilled the law in every respect. Every jot and tittle of the whole law given at Mount Sinai was fulfilled, ended, and abolished in Christ. It was *"done away"* by Him in His life, death, and resurrection, with a New Testament or covenant being brought about (Acts 15:5-29; Rom. 10:4; II Cor. 3:6-15; Gal. 3:19-25; 4:21-31; 5:1-5, 18; Eph. 2:15; Col. 2:14-17; Heb. 7:11-28; 8:6-13; 9:1-22; 10:1-18). In fact, Jesus is the new covenant, whereas the Cross of Christ is the meaning of that covenant, the meaning of which was given to the apostle Paul (Gal., Chpt. 1).

THE FOUNDATION OF THE NEW COVENANT

"Whosoever therefore shall break one of these least commandments, and shall teach men so, he shall be called the least in the kingdom of heaven: but whosoever shall do and teach them, the same shall be called great in the kingdom of heaven" (Mat. 5:19).

In verse 19, the Lord begins to lay down the foundation for the new covenant. As well, verses 18 and 19 proclaim the tremendous significance of the Word of God, whether the old covenant or the new, a significance, in fact, that is so great that it defies description.

Of course, the world not at all understands the absolute validity of the Word of God, and neither does most of the church. Even good Christians seldom understand how absolutely important it is in every respect.

Actually, the Word of God should be a lifelong project in the heart and life of every single believer. Inasmuch as it is the Word of God, and there is no other in the world and, consequently, the only revealed truth in the world, it should be studied diligently by every believer until its contents are thoroughly mastered, at least as the Lord helps one to do so. In all fairness and honesty, inasmuch as it is the Word of God, I think I can say without fear of contradiction that it is impossible for one to exhaust its teaching and knowledge.

The word *"whosoever"* lays the ground of impartiality for all and, as well, lays the Word of God as the foundation of all teaching and instruction.

I personally think that without a proper understanding of the Cross of Christ, which made it possible for the entire human race (at least those who believe) to be brought back into a right-standing relationship with God, one cannot really understand the new covenant. This is true especially when one considers that the Cross of Christ is the meaning of the new covenant.

The Cross—what Jesus there did—made redemption the foundation of human life, that is, He made a way for every person to have forgiveness of sins and fellowship with God.

COMMANDMENTS

The phrase, *"Whosoever therefore shall break one of these least commandments,"* concerns the abrogation of any part of the Word of God, even that thought to be the least significant!

This passage does not speak of a lack of light on a given biblical subject, but instead, a direct denial of the Word of God fostered by unbelief. In fact, no one has all the light on the Bible, but all must hunger and thirst for more light to be given. As well, one must have a desire to be corrected by the Holy Spirit with whatever method He chooses.

The Word of God is such that if men allow leaven to creep in, unless the leaven is removed, it will ultimately corrupt the whole. Consequently, the believer should constantly pray that the Holy Spirit *"leads me in the paths of righteousness for His name's sake"* (Ps. 23:3).

If self-will enters into our study and understanding of the Bible, the Lord will allow a judicial blindness to settle upon such people. However, if we study it with the intention of it correcting us, the Holy Spirit will superintend its direction of truth within our lives because the Word is truth (Jn. 17:17).

A LITTLE LEAVEN

As an example, if a church body, such as a religious denomination, allows error to creep in and allows that error to become a part of its belief structure, it will ultimately color and corrupt the entirety of all that is believed. That's what Paul was talking about when he said: *"A little leaven* (corruption) *leavens* (corrupts) *the whole lump"* (Gal. 5:9). That's an extremely serious statement, and we should take it to heart.

For instance, the unscriptural doctrine of unconditional eternal security, as it is embraced by many Baptists and many others, pretty well colors the entirety of their theology. Consequently, the *"little leaven,"* and we say it once again, has now leavened the whole lump.

This does not mean that one cannot be saved and, thereby, believe in the doctrine of unconditional eternal security because salvation is a matter of trusting Christ and not doctrinal perfection, or even the correct understanding of all peripheral doctrines of Scripture. And yet, any erroneous understanding definitely does weaken our daily walk and advancement in Christ. Consequently, the phrase, *"And shall teach men so, he shall be called the least in the kingdom of heaven,"* means to flat-out disbelieve parts of the Bible. *"He shall be called the least,"* means that the reward he could have had, he will not have.

DAMNABLE DOCTRINES

And yet, there are certain doctrines that people claim to get from the Bible, or else, they just devise these doctrines out of their own minds, that can lead a person to be eternally lost. As an example, many have asked if an individual can disbelieve the virgin birth of Christ and still be saved.

No, they cannot simply because to disbelieve that strikes at the very heart of God's plan of salvation for the human family and denies the faith that saves. This is basically that of which Paul was speaking in Hebrews, Chapters 6 and 10. Both chapters speak of rejecting the atoning work of Christ in which one must believe in order to be saved. If that is denied, there is no way for one to be saved.

The same is true for evolution—one cannot believe such a fabrication and be saved.

It is certainly true that some new converts may not have light on certain subjects, and to be sure, the Holy Spirit will be patient. Nevertheless, one will definitely line up with the Word of God respecting soul-saving subjects if he is to be saved.

So as not to cause misunderstanding, we are speaking of subjects that pertain to the fundamentals of the faith and not to peripheral subjects, although extremely important.

ALL TRUTH

As another example, if a Catholic truly makes Christ his or her Saviour and not the church, the Holy Spirit will invariably lead the individual out of that system because it is His purpose to always *"guide you into all truth"* (Jn. 16:13).

Even though my statement is blunt, I must say it: After coming to Christ, one cannot remain in the Catholic Church, embracing its erroneous tenets of faith, and be saved! The entire fabric of Catholic belief is contrary to the Word of God. If we are to use the Word of God as the rule of faith, which we certainly must do, it is impossible to wed the two.

The phrase, *"But whosoever shall do and teach them,"* concerns one making the Word of God his rule of faith for salvation and nothing else.

The phrase, *"The same shall be called great in the kingdom of heaven,"* means that the Lord sets the Bible as the standard of all righteousness and that He recognizes no other.

THE CONTRAST

"For I say unto you, that except your righteousness shall exceed the righteousness of the scribes and Pharisees, you shall in no case enter into the kingdom of heaven" (Mat. 5:20).

The absolute necessity of the new birth is here declared as imperative in every case.

The phrase, *"For I say unto you,"* is meant to be in contrast to the scribes and Pharisees. In other words, there was a direct clash respecting the teaching of the Bible, with Christ claiming His Word as law and gospel and, as well, denouncing the teaching of the Pharisees, which He later called *"leaven"* (Mat. 16:11-12).

Consequently, even at the very beginning, one can see the animosity that could not help but intensify between Christ and the religious leaders of Israel. Once again we go back to the Cross. I think that one cannot really understand the Bible as one should unless one understands the Cross of Christ, not only as it relates to our salvation, but also, our sanctification.

The Cross was not something that just happened to Jesus— He came to die. The Cross was His purpose in coming. He is *"the Lamb slain from the foundation of the world"* (Rev. 13:8). The incarnation of Christ would have no meaning without the Cross.

RIGHTEOUSNESS

The phrase, *"That except your righteousness shall exceed the righteousness of the scribes and Pharisees,"* refers to two types of righteousness, which can be summed up in several categories.

The first type is self-righteousness, relative righteousness, and works righteousness.

Self-righteousness: This constitutes dependence on one's own ability and seeks to justify self on real or fancied grounds (Lk. 18:9). One must come to the realization that God is always justified, while man is always condemned.

Self-righteousness is always, and without exception, the result of faith in something other than the Cross of Christ. Irrespective as to what direction it takes, if it's not the Cross, it will lead to self-righteousness every time. So, due to the paucity of preaching and teaching on the Cross at this present time, the modern church can probably be said to be the most self-righteous church that ever was, at least since the Reformation.

Relative righteousness: this *"righteousness"* compares itself to others and always finds some whom it thinks is of less stature than itself, hence, the Pharisee claiming, *"I am not as other men are, extortioners, unjust, adulterers, or even as this publican"* (Lk. 18:11).

This type of righteousness, as self-righteousness, is practiced by all of the world and most of the church. However, comparing our righteousness with others is entirely the wrong measuring rod. The standard is Christ and not others. When compared with Him, our answer can be only as Isaiah, *"Woe is me"* (Isa. 6:5), as Job, *"Behold, I am vile"* (Job 40:4), and as John on the isle of Patmos when he saw Christ in His glorified form, *"I fell at His feet as dead"* (Rev. 1:17).

Works righteousness: This once again goes back to the parable of the Pharisee and publican, with the Pharisee extolling his good works, *"I fast twice in the week, I give tithes of all* *that I possess"* (Lk. 18:12). Regrettably, most all of the world and the church depend on this type of righteousness, which God will never accept!

The second type of righteousness is imputed righteousness. **Imputed righteousness** is the only righteousness that God will accept.

Imputed righteousness is the righteousness freely imputed by Christ to all who place their faith exclusively in Him and what He has done for us at the Cross. The publican (criminal) is used as an example, *"And the publican, standing afar off, would not lift up so much as his eyes unto heaven, but smote upon his breast, saying, God be merciful to me a sinner."*

Jesus said, *"I tell you, this man went down to his house justified rather than the other: for every one who exalts himself shall be abased; and he who humbles himself shall be exalted"* (Lk. 18:13-14).

Imputed righteousness is something the believer does not deserve and, in fact, can do nothing to earn it. It is given freely by grace.

In other words, one might say that the only qualification for this type of righteousness is to be unqualified and know it!

However, let it be also understood that it is the Cross of Christ and our faith in that finished work that opens the door for this righteousness to be freely given to us. To be sure, it will be freely given to anyone who evidences faith in Christ and what He did for us at the Cross.

"For by grace are you saved through faith; and that not of your- selves: it is the gift of God: Not of works, lest any man should

boast. For we are His workmanship, created in Christ Jesus unto good works, which God has before ordained that we should walk in them" (Eph. 2:8-10).

THE KINGDOM OF HEAVEN

The phrase, *"You shall in no case enter into the kingdom of heaven,"* loudly proclaims that there is only one type of righteousness that God will accept. It is the righteousness that is freely given by Christ to all who will agree that they have none themselves and, in fact, cannot obtain any righteousness by their own ability and are not worthy of any. This is the reason that it is so difficult for most people to be saved.

Most establish their own standards for salvation—standards that basically balance the good against the bad. It is a standard that God will not accept. Consequently, most of the world has died lost, and most are dying lost at present.

THE LAW OF MOSES

"You have heard that it was said by them of old time, You shall not kill; and whosoever shall kill shall be in danger of the judgment" (Mat. 5:21).

The phrase, *"You have heard that it was said by them of old time,"* refers back to the law of Moses.

The Lord is now going to compare the new covenant, for which He is laying the foundation, to the old covenant. To be sure, it will far exceed the old in demands and penalties; however, whereas the old looked to the individual, the new looks entirely to Christ. It is all found in the Cross.

Actually, the Cross is the central event in time and eternity and the answer to all the problems of both. The Cross is not the cross of a man but the Cross of God, and it can never be fully comprehended through human experience. The Cross is God exhibiting His nature.

COMMANDMENTS

The short phrase, *"You shall not kill,"* should have been translated, "You shall do no murder"; for the magistrate is ordered by God to put capital offenders to death (Gen. 9:6; Rom. 13:1-6).

MODERN TECHNOLOGY AND ABORTION

The awfulness and the wickedness of abortion know no bounds. To be sure, this nation is going to pay, and pay dearly, for the fact that it murders millions of innocents, some as late as nine months, in other words, ready to be born.

Modern technology can and does show the growth of the baby from conception. So, the idea that it's only a blob of flesh is a lie indeed! Pure and simple, abortion is murder. We can call it whatever we like, and we can try to dress it up, but murder is what God says about it. Little by little in this nation of America, we are losing our way, with the great foundations of the faith being steadily eroded. The blame can be laid at the feet of the church.

ANGER

"But I say unto you, that whosoever is angry with his brother without a cause shall be in danger of the judgment: and whosoever shall say to his brother, Raca, shall be in danger of the council: but whosoever shall say, You fool, shall be in danger of hell fire" (Mat. 5:22).

The phrase, *"But I say unto you,"* is emphatic, with the Lord once again making Himself the authority. He was the authority and was made such by the Holy Spirit. As such, the Bible and Christ are the same. The former is the written Word, while the latter is the living Word. As such, they are indivisible.

The phrase, *"That whosoever is angry with his brother without a cause shall be in danger of the judgment,"* places unjust anger in the same category as murder. Consequently, Jesus addresses not only the act but the source from which it springs, i.e., the evil heart.

The next two statements are meant to contrast the Jewish law with the law of God.

Once again, we go back to the Cross: The Cross of Christ is the gate through which any and every individual can enter into oneness with God. It is not a gate we pass right through. It is one where we abide in the light that is found there, and forever. In fact, the heart of salvation is the Cross of Christ.

RACA

The phrase, *"And whosoever shall say to his brother, Raca, shall be in danger of the council,"* has reference to the Jewish Sanhedrin, which was composed of 71 judges and was presided over by the high priest, or it was a local council of each synagogue, which was composed of three or more men.

The word, *Raca,* was a word used to describe severe contention between parties, with the situation deteriorating to the point of bodily harm. Such, as is obvious, would find themselves in a court of law, as is here described.

A FOOL

Jesus said, *"But whosoever shall say, You fool, shall be in danger of hell fire,"* but yet, Jesus Himself repeatedly called people fools as is recorded in Matthew and Luke.

In the chapter that we are now studying (Mat., Chpt. 5), where Jesus forbade the use of that kind of accusation, the Greek word translated "fool" is *moros,* which means "a wicked reprobate, destitute of all spirituality." This, in effect, consigned a person to hell. No one but God has the right to pass that kind of judgment.

However, in Luke, Chapter 11, and in Matthew, Chapter 23, the word *fool* in the Greek is a totally different word. It is *aphron,* which means "senseless ones without reason; foolish; stupid; acting without intelligence." So, I think it's fairly obvious that Jesus was not saying the same in Matthew, Chapter 5, as He was saying in Matthew, Chapter 23, and Luke, Chapter 11.

Our English word *fool* was used in each instance, but it meant two different things altogether in the Greek, the language in which the original text was written. The problem then was with the translation from one language to another. Often, the only way to resolve these complex difficulties is to study the text of Scripture in the original Greek and Hebrew languages. We may have trouble understanding the context of a passage, or a translator may have been imperfect in his choice of words, but the Bible itself is error-free.

THE ALTAR

"Therefore if you bring your gift to the altar, and there remember that your brother has ought against you" (Mat. 5:23).

The phrase, *"Therefore if you bring your gift to the altar,"* is meant to refer to the brazen altar as used in the offering of sacrifices in the law of Moses.Because Jesus was speaking to Jews, He would use the terminology of the old covenant, i.e., the altar; however, under the new covenant, it would have reference to one coming before the Lord and asking forgiveness for wrongdoing. Consequently, the statement is of extreme importance!

"And there remember that your brother has ought against you," is meant to describe our relationship with our fellowman. In other words, if we hold unforgiveness in our hearts toward others, our petition to the Lord for forgiveness on His part cannot be brought about until reconciliation is made with the offended party, that is, if it's possible. This, in effect, goes along with Christ's statement, *"For if you forgive men their trespasses, your heavenly Father will also forgive you: But if you forgive not men their trespasses, neither will your Father forgive your trespasses"* (Mat. 6:14-15).

The idea is that the Lord has forgiven us of so much, and considering that, how can we fail to forgive others?

THE GIFT

"Leave there your gift before the altar, and go your way; first be reconciled to your brother, and then come and offer your gift" (Mat. 5:24).

The phrase, *"Leave there your gift before the altar,"* is meant to put first things first. In other words, the intimation is that the Lord will not accept our gift unless we do all within our power to make things right with the offended party.

This makes Christianity superior to all religions. Once again, the idea is that the heart be addressed and that if the heart is truly addressed, it will be kept free from guilt toward one's fellowman.

"And go your way," refers to making whatever effort is necessary to bring about this reconciliation, as stated, if at all possible.

"First be reconciled to your brother," emphasizes the significance that God places on right relationships with others. Of course, there are some situations that cannot be reconciled due to one or more parties not desiring such. God does not hold us accountable in such cases but does hold us accountable to make every effort.

"And then come and offer your gift," has reference to the personal relationship being handled first, or at least doing all within our power to do so, and *"then"* the Lord will hear our prayers and forgive us if, in fact, forgiveness is necessary.

Sadly, most Christians little heed these commands, even though they strike at the very heart of that which we call Christianity. As a result, many prayers and petitions to the Lord go unanswered, and many sins remain unforgiven.

It is a sobering thought!

THE WORD OF CHRIST

"Agree with your adversary quickly, while you are in the way with him; lest at any time the adversary deliver you to the judge, and the judge deliver you to the officer, and you be cast into prison" (Mat. 5:25).

Many misunderstand verses 25 and 26, thinking they pertain to legal matters and the need to settle before going to court. However, that is not the intention of Christ, as these two verses relate to verses 23 and 24, and in a way, to verses 21 and 22, as well.

The idea as tendered by Christ is that offenses against man are here represented in their true character as offenses against God, who is, therefore, depicted as the adversary in a lawsuit. As well, He is also depicted as the judge and that His decision will be rendered in a very disagreeable manner if His Word is not followed.

THE JUDGE

The phrase, *"Agree with your adversary quickly, while you are in the way with him,"* refers to the absolute necessity of making doubly certain that one's fellowman is treated right. This is an absolute requirement by Christ. To offend a brother is to offend Christ and is here made glaringly evident.

"Lest at any time the adversary deliver you to the judge," refers to one's unscriptural actions delivering him to the judge, i.e., the Lord Jesus Christ.

An example is Moses who fell on his face before the Lord when Korah, Dathan, and Abram led a rebellion against him, as is recorded in Numbers, Chapter 16. The unholy trio was dealing with Moses, but they quickly found themselves dealing with the Lord, who is the righteous judge.

The phrase, *"And the judge deliver you to the officer, and you be cast into prison,"* in effect, refers to a spiritual judgment, which is the worst of all! Consequently, millions of Christians are presently in prison, at least in a spiritual sense, simply because they have harmed their brother or sister in the Lord and have not sought to make it right. To offend the one who belongs to God is to offend God.

The prison can consist of sickness, poverty, or any number of things devised by the Lord.

GOD'S WAY

"Verily I say unto you, You shall by no means come out thence, till you have paid the uttermost farthing" (Mat. 5:26).

I think the idea is glaringly obvious in verse 26!

If wrongdoing is carried out against a fellow believer, upon proper repentance before the Lord and with proper restitution to the individual, the matter, as proclaimed in verses 23 and 24, can be handled readily and without penalty. However, failure to do so—sadly the case much, if not most, of the time—invites extremely harsh penalties.

The phrase, *"Verily I say unto you,"* is meant to impress upon the reader the absolute solemnity of this statement as given by Christ.

The phrase, *"You shall by no means come out thence,"* means that if God's way (repentance and seeking of forgiveness from the offended party) is not entered into, the consequences will be dire indeed!

It is impossible to deal with holiness until, at the same time, we deal with sin, which can only be dealt with at the Cross.

Sin is a fundamental relationship; it is not wrongdoing so much as it is wrong *being*.

Sin is deliberate and determined independence from God.

PAYMENT

The phrase, *"Till you have paid the uttermost farthing,"* concerns itself with payment in installments. In other words, there will not be just one reverse, but one after the other, and with no end in sight. This applies not only to matters between believers but, as well, entire religious denominations. There is no license given in the Word of God for anyone to mistreat someone else, irrespective of whom they may be!

The other day, a very able lawyer spoke to me concerning a major religious denomination. He said, "Brother Swaggart, until the leadership of this denomination makes things right, the problems they are now experiencing will only exacerbate." He was right; the debt draws interest, and, in effect, the payments never end.

As Christ here defines, how so much easier it is (if, in fact, one has been wronged) for the offending party to simply say in sincerity, "I have wronged you; would you please forgive me? I will do whatever I can to make restitution before God and man." The statement just made constitutes only a few simple words, but it is so difficult for most to carry out.

Amazing grace—how sweet the sound
That saved a wretch like me!
I once was lost, but now am found—
Was blind, but now I see.

THE SERMON
on the
MOUNT

CHAPTER 3

THE STATE OF
THE HEART

THE STATE OF THE HEART

"YOU HAVE HEARD THAT it was said by them of old time, You shall not commit adultery. But I say unto you, that whosoever looks on a woman to lust after her has committed adultery with her already in his heart" (Mat. 5:27-28).

ADULTERY

The believer's conduct toward his fellowman continues with Jesus' command respecting divorce and remarriage.

As well, He addresses the true intent of the law, which was completely different from the interpretation of the Pharisees.

The commandment, *"You shall not commit adultery,"* is the seventh of the Ten Commandments (Ex. 20:14).

The Christian faith bases everything on the extreme, self-confident nature of sin. Other so-called faiths deal with sins—the Bible alone deals with *sin.*

The first thing Jesus confronted in people was the heredity of sin. It is because we have ignored this in our presentation of the gospel that the message of the gospel has lost its explosive power.

The revealed truth of the Bible is not that Jesus Christ took on Himself our fleshly sins, but that He took on Himself the heredity of sin that no man can even touch, which speaks of original sin that began with Adam.

BEHAVIOR

The law of Moses was based on behavior, which is as all law directed toward the act itself. However, the new covenant is far more stringent than the old because it directs attention to the heart of the individual instead of the act.

The phrase, *"But I say unto you,"* does not deny the law of Moses, but rather takes it to its conclusion, which could only be done by Christ. In other words, the old covenant pointed the way to the new covenant, which came with Christ. In fact, Christ is the new covenant (I Cor. 10:4).

DIVORCE

As well, the Pharisees were continuously arguing over the divorce question, and now, by His statement, Jesus settled the issue completely, at least for His followers. He took it much further than the act itself and directed attention to the heart, which gives birth to the act.

In retrospect, the law, at least in some measure, did actually go beyond the act, even directing attention to the heart by the tenth commandment, *"You shall not covet"* (Ex. 20:17). In other words, the tenth commandment said that not only must the act (whatever infraction) not be committed, but, as well, the individual must not even have a desire to do so.

The word *desire* is used in the sense of one wanting to do something and, in fact, would do it if the occasion presented itself and could be done without being found out.

THE TRUE NATURE OF ADULTERY

The phrase, *"That whosoever looks on a woman to lust after her,"* means to look at one in order to lust and with a look that stimulates the lust. It is not merely looking at someone with a temptation crossing the mind, but instead, it is with a desire to carry it out if the consequences can be avoided.

"Has committed adultery with her already in his heart," is a serious charge indeed! It means that God chalks it up as if the sin were committed. Quite possibly, Christ was directing His attention not only to the general public, and for all time, but, as well, to a sect called the "bleeding Pharisees."

THE BLEEDING PHARISEES

These individuals wore a heavy bandage around their foreheads because they walked about, at least much of the time, with their eyes closed and would, consequently, bump into objects, especially with their heads, hence, they were called "bleeding Pharisees." They were doing so, at least they said, to keep from looking at members of the opposite sex, which made others think of them as extremely holy.

Despite Jesus using the word *look,* He was, in effect, saying that the sin is in the heart and not the eyes. Therefore, His statement must have angered them greatly as it completely blew away their hypotheses.

THAT WHICH OFFENDS YOU

"And if your right eye offend you, pluck it out, and cast it from you: for it is profitable for you that one of your members should perish, and not that your whole body should be cast into hell. And if your right hand offend you, cut it off, and cast it from you: for it is profitable for you that one of your members should perish, and not that your whole body should be cast into hell" (Mat. 5:29-30).

The Lord does not intend for His statement to be taken literally as He has already explained that the offense is not in the eye or hand, but instead, the heart! In effect, a blind man can lust.

The idea is that sin is so bad, with the possibility of such damning the soul, that drastic action must be taken to subdue such passions. In other words, if by plucking out our eyes such could save our souls, it would be well worth the drastic action; however, this is not what Jesus was saying.

As well, if we think these sins are seldom committed, and by few, we are of all people most mistaken. In fact, the areas mentioned by Christ in this Sermon on the Mount (which covers Matthew, Chapters 5 through 7) address every major life concern. Therefore, in the aggregate, it is something with which all grapple on a continuing basis.

"For it is profitable for you," proves the necessity of obeying God in these matters and, as well, allowing Him to set the standard rather than man.

The seriousness of this matter is emphasized in the first phrase, *"And if your right eye offend you, pluck it out, and cast it from you."*

HELL

Adultery was once a crime in America because the law of man was based on the law of God. However, the Bible is no longer the standard for moral measurement in America, and consequently, man's laws change with each administration. And yet, making such into a law does not solve the problem either. In fact, the problem can be solved only by the heart being changed, and that can only be done by a person accepting the Lord Jesus Christ as his Saviour and making Him the Lord of his life.

"And not that your whole body should be cast into hell," unequivocally lets man know just how serious these matters are, and more particularly, there is most definitely a place called "hell."

Regrettably, most modern preachers do not even believe there is a hell despite the Words of Christ.

For the Lord to say something once signifies its importance. For Him to say it twice, as here, signifies its extreme importance!

The Lord's method of teaching was symbolic and figurative. It is better to destroy what tempts to wrongdoing, though it is as precious as an eye or a hand, than to suffer eternal torments. However, as we've already stated, the Lord is showing to us the seriousness of the matter. The sin is not in the eye or the hand, with that being neutral, but rather the heart (Rom. 6:13).

Few people on earth presently believe verses 29 and 30, while every single person in hell now believes it readily!

DIVORCE

"It has been said, Whosoever shall put away his wife, let him give her a writing of divorcement: But I say unto you, that whosoever shall put away his wife, saving for the cause of fornication, causes her to commit adultery: and whosoever shall marry her who is divorced commits adultery" (Mat. 5:31-32).

"It has been said," refers to Deuteronomy 24:1-4.

"Whosoever shall put away his wife," refers to divorce proceedings.

"Let him give her a writing of divorcement," now placed the emphasis on this legal form. Jesus would change that by dealing with the very heart of the problem.

"But I say unto you," is once again designed to settle the matter once and for all. As such, and even though incarnate, He placed Himself in the position of deity, which He was, meaning that proper attention must be given to His statements.

"That whosoever shall put away his wife," places the emphasis on the seriousness of this matter, which was far above any and all legal forms. In effect, and due to the fact that divorce strikes at the very heart of the family, great attention is given to it by Christ. If it is not followed to the letter, catastrophe on a nationwide or even worldwide scale is the result.

All of this shows the sin of man.

God made His own Son *"to be sin,"* that is, "a sin offering," that He might make the sinner into a saint.

It is revealed throughout the Bible that our Lord took on Himself the sin of the world through *identification* with us, not through *sympathy* for us. He deliberately took on His own shoulders and endured in His own body the complete, cumulative sin of the human race.

FORNICATION

"Saving for the cause of fornication, causes her to commit adultery," gives the only allowance for divorce, with the exception of the second allowance as referred to by Paul in I Corinthians 7:10-11.

The words *"put away"* mean divorce, and they were so understood by the Jews. If the divorce was granted for fornication, a sin God looked upon as most serious, the putting away was legal and sanctioned by Christ. It made the contract null and void as before marriage.

Many people misunderstand the true meaning of adultery and fornication. They think fornication applies only to single people, while adultery applies to those who are married. Such thinking is scripturally wrong. Adultery is the unlawful relationship between men and women, single or married. In fact, all fornication is adultery, but all adultery is not fornication.

As an example, David was an adulterer, but he was not a fornicator as Esau was (Heb. 12:16).

- Fornication in the Bible means "adultery of married or single people, committed over and over again with different partners" (Mat. 19:9; I Cor. 7:2; 10:8; I Thess. 4:3; Rev. 9:21).

- It also refers to incest (I Cor. 5:1; 10:8).

- It, as well, refers to idolatry, which speaks of adultery in honor of idol gods (II Chron. 21:11; Isa. 23:17; Ezek. 16:15, 26, 29; Acts 15:20, 29; 21:25; Rev. 2:14-21; 14:8; 17:2-4; 18:3-9; 19:2).

- As well, it refers to homosexuality and male prostitution (Rom. 1:24-29; I Cor. 6:9-11; II Cor. 12:21; Gal. 5:19; Eph. 5:3; Col. 3:5; Heb. 12:16; Jude, Vss. 6-7).

"And whosoever shall marry her who is divorced commits adultery," means one who is divorced with no scriptural grounds.

For a more detailed account of this important subject of divorce and remarriage, please see commentary on Malachi, Chapter 2 in The Expositor's Study Bible.

SWEAR NOT AT ALL

"Again, you have heard that it has been said by them of old time, You shall not forswear yourself, but shall perform unto the Lord your oaths: But I say unto you, Swear not at all; neither by heaven; for it is God's throne: Nor by the earth; for it is His footstool: neither

by Jerusalem; for it is the city of the great King. Neither shall you swear by your head, because you cannot make one hair white or black" (Mat. 5:33-36).

As verses 21 through 26 had to do with the sixth commandment, *"You shall not kill"* (murder) (Ex. 20:13), and verses 27 through 32 had to do with the seventh commandment, *"You shall not commit adultery"* (Ex. 20:14), verses 33 through 37 have to do with the third commandment, *"You shall not take the name of the Lord your God in vain"* (Ex. 20:7).

"Again, you have heard that it has been said by them of old time," once again alludes to tradition.

Over and over again, Jesus used terms such as, *"You have heard,"* or *"It has been said,"* meaning that the Word of God had been twisted to mean something it did not say. This has ever been the case with professors of religion.

In reality, most of the people in Israel did not know the Bible, and even most of those who did attempted to make it fit their beliefs instead of allowing it to mold their beliefs. It has little changed presently!

"You shall not forswear yourself, but shall perform unto the Lord your oaths," concerns that which was commonly done among the people. Consequently, by their actions, they made the Lord a part of their exaggerations, lies, and fabrications.

VOWS

"But I say unto you, Swear not at all," has nothing to do with profanity, at least in this case, but rather the making of vows

by heaven, earth, or any other thing, in other words, to swear by these things.

The idea of these verses is that it had become commonplace for individuals to pull God's name into their declarations. It was done in a flippant, light, and irresponsible manner. This is what the Lord was forbidding.

It does not refer to solemn oaths that must be taken in some circumstances, such as courts of law, etc. Actually, the apostle Paul took oaths in his writings (II Cor. 1:23; 11:31).

Once again, we emphasize that the Lord was addressing Himself to the wholesale use of His name in whatever capacity respecting ordinary conversation, etc. In fact, modern Christians also fall into this same trap.

Sin is so prevalent and so easy—to commit it makes the cause of all human problems. God made His Son who knew no sin to be sin for us. By so doing, He placed salvation for the entire human race solely on the basis of the Cross.

Jesus Christ reconciled the human race and put it back to where God designed it to be, and did so by the means of the Cross. Now anyone can experience that reconciliation—being brought into oneness with God—on the basis of what our Lord has done on the Cross.

PROFANING THE NAME OF THE LORD

Many Christians profane the name of God by exclaiming, "My God," upon hearing either some type of unusual announcement or attempting to make their statement stronger.

Others use the phrase, "By God," once again, taking an oath in flippant conversation, or else, in anger. Others use the name "Jesus Christ" in a flippant exclamation, which is meant to express surprise, etc.

As well, outright profanity has become so common over television and in normal usage that many Christians are not offended by it anymore, or at least raise little objection. As a consequence, many Christians think little of using the expletives "damn" or "hell" in expressing themselves. They think it lends weight to their statements. They don't stop to realize that these two words, plus others of similar comport, are, in effect, words describing acts of God or places of designation created by God.

At any rate, it is swearing, pure and simple, and is absolutely forbidden by the Lord. His name is to be regarded, respected, revered, and held above all such thinking, and especially conversation. The failure to do such shows an improper relationship with Him, with little understanding as to exactly who He is, the Creator and Redeemer, and who exactly we are, the created and, therefore, absolutely dependent upon Him.

COMMUNICATION

"But let your communication be, Yes, yes; No, no: for whatsoever is more than these comes of evil" (Mat. 5:37).

"But let your communication be, Yes, yes; No, no," is meant to express the following: The word of the believer should be such that it seldom requires an oath to substantiate what is being said. If one says, "Yes," it means yes. If one says, "No," it means no.

It is regrettable that such responsible truthfulness is little adhered to anymore! When the Bible was adhered to more fully, a man's word was his bond. Now, at least in most cases, a man's word, even among believers, means little!

Christ is here stating that His followers must stand out by their truthfulness, honesty, and integrity.

"For whatsoever is more than these comes of evil," is meant to say that if yes does not mean yes, or no does not mean no, evil is then the result.

Regrettably, even among many Christians, evil is the result more so than righteousness!

YOU HAVE HEARD

"You have heard that it has been said, An eye for an eye, and a tooth for a tooth" (Mat. 5:38).

Someone has said that this phrase more accurately describes the spirit of Mosaic legislation than any other!

Even though this admonition was seldom carried out, by the time of Christ, it was almost nonexistent, with such infractions most often handled by the payment of money.

Even though there were jails in those days, still, many, if not most things of this nature were handled in a different manner than incarceration. The guilty party was made to pay either in money or in work on behalf of the injured party.

By using the phrase again, *"You have heard that it has been said,"* Christ was attempting to pull Israel away from the letter of the law to the Spirit of the law.

TURN THE OTHER CHEEK

"But I say unto you, that you resist not evil: but whosoever shall smite you on the right cheek, turn to him the other also" (Mat. 5:39).

"But I say unto you, that you resist not evil," is not meant to refer to the official duties of governments, but instead, is meant to address the individual believer. In fact, if evil is not resisted by government, anarchy is the result. Actually, government, as ordained by God, is said to be, *"The minister of God, a revenger to execute wrath upon him who does evil"* (Rom. 13:4).

"But whosoever shall smite you on the right cheek, turn to him the other also," is meant to be taken figuratively. In fact, the offering of the other cheek may be done outwardly, while the opposite is in the heart. Only if it is done inwardly can it always be right.

Actually, when the Lord was smitten on the cheek (Jn. 18:22-23), He did not turn the other cheek, but with dignity, rebuked the assailant.

The idea of these passages is that the heavenly citizen is not to be ready to take offense (v. 39), nor prompt to go to law (v. 40), disobliging (v. 41), heartless (v. 42), or revengeful (v. 44), but like his Father in heaven, he is to be kind to both evil and good men. So, in that sense, he is to be perfect as His Father in heaven in that his actions will correspond.

PERSONAL DEFENSE

"And if any man will sue you at the law, and take away your coat, let him have your cloak also" (Mat. 5:40).

Once again, this Scripture is not meant to be obeyed in the literal sense, for Paul, at least in the literal sense, did the opposite. When the Jews were determined to hold court on him in Jerusalem, he said, *"I stand at Caesar's judgment seat, where I ought to be judged"* (Acts 25:10).

As a Roman, which Paul was, he had the right to do this. In other words, he did not take the position that whatever you want to do to me, you may do! In effect, he *"resisted this evil,"* as he should have done.

The idea of these verses is that we not be so quick to try to defend ourselves, but instead, place the situation in the hands of the Lord.

And yet, there are times, as we have attempted to bring out, that the spirit of these commands as given by Christ will be kept totally, while at times, the actions are forced otherwise. In other words, in our country of the United States, if someone sues us, we have no choice but to defend ourselves. It's not something we want to do or desire to do, nor is it something that we have agitated, but it's something over which we have no control.

In all of this we see the frailty of man along with the grace and power of God. For instance, a man cannot redeem himself; redemption is the work of God and is absolutely finished and complete, and is done so by the Cross.

Its application to individual people is a matter of their own individual actions or responses to it.

A distinction must always be made between the revealed truth of redemption and the actual conscious experience of salvation in a person's life.

PAUL

Attempting to keep the letter of Christ's statements, Paul could have easily stated that if the Jews desired to try him in a court of law in Jerusalem (before the Sanhedrin), they were welcome to do so. However, that was not God's will inasmuch as they were only seeking to kill Paul. Consequently, while continuing to love them, despite their gross evil, he took advantage of Roman law by appealing to Caesar, which, as a Roman citizen, he had the right to do.

And yet, Paul, at the same time and by the action of the Holy Spirit, absolutely forbade Christians to go to court against other Christians in front of unbelievers. In other words, he forbade believers to initiate legal action against another fellow Christian (I Cor. 6:1-8). However, the Holy Spirit through him did not say anything about those who were not Christians. As well, there are many who claim to be Christians who really aren't.

THE HEART OF MAN

"And whosoever shall compel you to go a mile, go with him two" (Mat. 5:41).

Once again, let's see what this does not mean.

As is known, Rome ruled in Christ's day. Consequently, the soldiers were sometimes harsh, demanding that citizens, at times, carry baggage, etc.

Christ was not meaning that at times of such actions, the individual should carry the baggage the distance demanded and then carefully measure off an added similar distance, and when he was done, congratulate himself on the fulfilling of this command. To do so would completely misdirect the intention of the teaching of Christ.

The idea was that the believer was to have a good attitude and spirit and seek to be helpful and kind at all times, even under the most adverse circumstances. This is what Christ was teaching, and not the measurement of some distance, etc.

The entirety of the idea had to do with the heart of man and not so much his outward actions, but that which most surely would guide his actions accordingly.

THE TRUE SPIRIT

"Give to him who asks of you, and from him who would borrow of you turn not you away" (Mat. 5:42).

The idea of verse 42 is that the child of God should walk in fellowship with the Father and to imitate Him. For example, we are to help those of our fellowmen whom God would help and to help them, at least the best we can, in the same way.

And yet, we are not, for example, to give money to lazy people who won't work. The Holy Spirit through Paul said, *"If any would not work, neither should he eat"* (II Thess. 3:10).

Regrettably, many have attempted to turn these admonitions into rules and laws, which completely circumvent the true teaching of Christ. One can easily turn the other cheek outwardly, but only when he turns the other cheek inwardly can the true spirit of these admonitions be kept, which is intended by Christ.

HATRED

"You have heard that it has been said, You shall love your neighbor, and hate your enemy" (Mat. 5:43).

Once again, the Lord resorted to the phrase, *"You have heard that it has been said,"* which refers to a twisting of Scripture to make it mean something that it really does not say.

"You shall love your neighbor, and hate your enemy," was probably derived from Exodus 17:14-16; Leviticus 19:17-18; and Deuteronomy 7:1-2; 23:3-6. As such, these Scriptures really do not say *"hate your enemy,"* but had to do with the actions of enemy nations toward Israel, which, if not stopped, would have circumvented the plan of God. Actually, it was the actions of these enemies of goodness and of righteousness that were to be *hated* with a holy hatred. Inasmuch as these *enemies* were determined to destroy the people of God, measures were commanded to be taken against them. However, it was definitely not supposed to degenerate into a personal hatred.

All of this is possible only by the believer placing his or her faith exclusively in Christ and the Cross. For the most part, the modern church needs to go back and rebuild its foundation. That foundation has to be the Cross of Christ.

Through the Cross comes salvation, the baptism with the Holy Spirit, divine healing, all blessings and prosperity, and all communion and fellowship with the Lord. In other words, the Cross of Christ is the means for all of these things to be given to us.

In essence, even though the Cross of Christ could be labeled a doctrine, still, it is actually the very foundation of the faith on which all doctrine is built. If this is not the case, then we will find that the doctrine is wrong.

MODERN TIMES

For instance, the wars fought in my lifetime, consisting of World War II and Korea, with possibly Vietnam at its beginning, were wars carried out in order to stop the encroachment of evil. When Hitler's death camps in Europe were opened, where some 6 million Jews were ruthlessly executed, then it became painfully obvious just exactly how evil these opponents were. As such, they had to be resisted, which fulfilled Romans 13:1-7.

And yet, as a believer, particular individuals in these foreign armies were not to be hated—only their evil and wicked actions.

THE TEACHING OF CHRIST

"But I say unto you, Love your enemies, bless them who curse you, do good to them who hate you, and pray for them who despitefully use you, and persecute you" (Mat. 5:44).

Once again, the phrase, *"But I say unto you,"* proclaims the true intent of the law as well as the command of Christ. The teaching of Christ on this subject was so contrary to what was presently being practiced, which was perversion of the law, that Christ's words were as revolutionary as anything could possibly be. When the Jews, and especially the religious leaders, heard these words, they must have been dumbfounded. The teaching of Christ was totally opposite of that being presently practiced, and, in effect, this one verse totally set true Christianity apart from all the religions of the world. Sadly, it is presently not too much practiced, even by professing believers, but still, these admonitions lie at the very heart of what true Christianity is all about.

When the Bible speaks of faith or believing, it is, without exception, speaking of faith in the finished work of Christ.

When it speaks of grace, hope, peace, or any such like terminology, always and without exception, these things come totally and completely to us through the Cross of Christ. In other words, the Cross of Christ is the means.

The entire sacrificial system of the Old Testament, which began at the very dawn of time (Gen., Chpt., 4), pointed totally and completely toward the coming Redeemer, who would bring salvation by the price paid at the Cross.

Four things are said in verse 44. They are: love your enemies, bless those who curse you, do good to them who hate you, and pray for them who despitefully use you and persecute you.

1. LOVE YOUR ENEMIES

Such a concept was unthinkable even among the Jews, much less among the heathen! Actually, the *"love"* spoken of here by Christ is the God kind of love, which totally transcends that which is called *"love"* by man. The phrase, *"For God so loved the world"* (Jn. 3:16), is speaking of a world that hated Him.

When Christ is accepted into the heart, the heart is changed, with the love of God being instilled, which gives the believer the capacity to love as God loves. Within oneself and abilities, such cannot be done! However, with the true born-again experience and Christ reigning supremely within one's life, such not only can be done but, in truth, will be done!

This is the only true answer to racism, bigotry, and prejudice.

CORRESPONDING ACTIONS

As well, it must be remembered that true love, as expressed in the heart, will find itself in corresponding action. In other words, it is not just love that is spoken loudly, as happens in most cases, but instead, it shows itself in actions.

Love awakened must find expression in a transformed lifestyle. The divine principle of love infuses the believer and moves Christians just as it moved God to love even enemies.

The New Testament explores in depth the impact of the divine love on our relationships in this world. Love creates a new community as brothers and sisters in Christ are bonded together.

Love prompts obedience and provides the motivation that moves believers to respond to the Lord.

Love transforms the character of the individual and provides a sense of purpose. Love stabilizes relationships, enabling us to overcome the tensions that shatter friendships.

A CONCERN FOR OTHERS

Love compels a practical concern for others that leads us to reach out and meet their needs. It is love that moves us toward the righteousness that law calls for but cannot produce.

The phrase, *"Love your enemies,"* has to do with all types of infractions. It speaks of those who wrong you in any capacity, or even children who disobey their parents, etc. Such, in whatever capacity, is to be responded to by love, while never condoning the wrongdoing. In other words, if we want to help someone change, let us love them as Jesus loves us and them.

However, true love will, at times, result in chastisement of the loved one, at least in cases of personal relationships, such as parents to children. The chastisement is to be carried out when needed because of love (Heb. 12:6).

Jesus was speaking here of individuals. While nations are not to hate their counterparts, still there are times that nations have to defend themselves, and have to use powerful force to overcome those who would take peace from the world. As it regards this, many have stated that the United States is not the policeman of the world. I beg to disagree! It *is* the policeman of the world.

Let me explain: America has this position, not so much because it asked for it, but simply because of the moral high ground this nation occupies, and that is solely because of biblical Christianity. Regrettably, we are losing that moral high ground because of forsaking the Word of God. If a war is just, it has to be fought. I speak of World War II. I speak, as well, of Korea. I speak now of the Muslim situation. Our leaders will regret it, and our nation will suffer if we do not realize that it is the religion of Islam that is causing the problem. While we may not be at war with this religion, it most definitely is at war with us. The quicker we realize this and take the appropriate steps, the better off we will be. Otherwise, the situation is going to increase more and more and take the lives of our young men and young ladies and, as well, take it to every strata of our society, which will bring this conflict to the very door of our homes in Anytown, USA. Unfortunately, our leaders have adopted the policy of "the good and bad Muslims." Regrettably, there are no good Muslims. All have sworn our destruction. To be frank, they hate America, and they hate Israel. Israel is referred to as the Little Satan and America as the Great Satan.

JOSEPH

And yet, to love someone who has greatly wronged us does not mean that we eagerly embrace that person. Joseph is a perfect example.

When his brothers stood before him in Egypt, not recognizing who he was, he did not immediately reveal himself to them. He made certain that they were changed before that revelation took place. Thank the Lord that there had been a change in their lives, which made it possible for him to show his love to them as he desired to do all along. However, if there had been no change in their lives, with murder still lurking in their hearts, the outcome of this scenario would have been far different.

2. BLESS THEM WHO CURSE YOU

This means that no matter how the believer is treated, we are to respond in a positive way and seek to introduce others to the life in Christ that brings blessing.

Incidentally, the word *curse*, as here used, does not refer to swearing or profanity. It refers to one who wishes you ill, hurt, or harm and would attempt to bring their wishes into a state of action if possible. Despite that, the true believer is absolutely forbidden to curse (wish harm upon) anyone.

James said, "*Therewith bless we God, even the Father; and therewith curse we men, which are made after the similitude of God. Out of the same mouth proceeds blessing and cursing. My brethren, these things ought not so to be*" (James 3:9-10).

The believer does have the capacity to curse, which will cause harm, especially because he is a believer; however, to do so is to take the God-given attributes of faith and love and pervert them, which sends bitter water out of a fountain that is supposed to send only sweet (James 3:11).

While causing momentary harm on the intended victim, the effect will ultimately destroy the perpetrator. Consequently, to fail to do what Christ here admonishes not only robs the victim of blessing but, as well, destroys the believer. The true Christian is designed by God to bless and not curse. To disobey is a perversion of the highest order.

BLESSING AND CURSING

Whenever believers bless those who curse them, they are unleashing upon those individuals the only power on earth that can truly change them. Therefore, the best and, in fact, only way to stop the adverse actions of such people is to truly bless them. Upon the advent of such blessing, the guilty party will either respond favorably, or else, rebel even further, consequently, destroying himself.

The actions and statements of a true believer are so powerful, at least in the spirit world, that either a positive or a negative effect is had on the individual or victim, even though unseen or unheard.

In other words, a blessing extended by a believer toward an individual, even though unknown by that individual, will be positively felt. They will be blessed and will sense it, even though they do not know the source. The same can be said in a negative way for curses.

A PERSONAL EXPERIENCE

Many times, if not all times, Frances and I have felt the negative response of fellow believers, even though we would not all the time be aware of the source. For instance, oftentimes, when feeling a tremendously heavy oppressive spirit on our persons, we would learn to watch for negative articles written by fellow believers, or some such device carried out against us. Of course, many times, especially if uttered by Christians on a worldwide basis, we would have no knowledge of the perpetrators but would definitely feel in our spirits the effects of the cursing.

James said, *"The tongue is a fire … Sets on fire the course of nature; and it is set on fire of hell"* (James 3:6).

To survive this, Frances and I have had to constantly, and gladly so, *"bless them who curse us."*

Thankfully, with some few, it has changed them, but sadly, with most, they have continued on their direction of cursing, which always results in ultimate destruction.

What does it mean to bless those who curse us?

To bless someone is to speak kindly of the person, irrespective of how they speak of you. It means to speak a positive word about them if at all possible.

And yet, Christ spoke very harshly of the Pharisees, even calling them hypocrites, serpents, and vipers (Mat. 23:29-33).

Was He violating His own Word?

No! Many modern believers have confused these issues, thinking it is wrong for preachers of the gospel to say anything negative concerning false doctrine or the propagators of such doctrine.

In truth, the Pharisees had spurned the love of God, refusing to be blessed, and had set themselves to destroy the gospel, therefore, causing many souls to be lost. As such, Christ, as all godly preachers, was obligated to point out not only the error of the false doctrine, which would cause many souls to be lost, but, as well, the perpetrators of that doctrine, at least the name of their group. To have not done so would have been a crime of the highest order, in effect, placing a seal of approval upon their lies and hypocrisy.

HUMAN GOVERNMENT

It is the same as the law of God in Romans 13:5, where it says, concerning human government, *"You must needs be subject."*

If human law abrogates God's law, the believer must not be subject to such law; however, one taking such a position must understand that there will be negative repercussions. God's law is a higher law, and all law must be subject to that law. So, believers in the early church did not violate the law of God when they refused to obey Caesar's law, which demanded that they call Caesar "Lord," etc.

Neither did Jesus violate His own law of loving one's enemies or blessing those who curse us by speaking of the Pharisees as He did! Neither do modern preachers of the gospel violate His law when they obey God in pointing out gross error and the perpetrators of such error, even in a very negative way, as Christ did.

Our Lord was speaking of individuals personally and wasn't speaking of those who perpetrate false doctrine, etc. That's a different story altogether.

Every single preacher we have named, we felt that he was preaching false doctrine in some area, and we felt that it had to be exposed. In no way did it mean that we hated or even disliked the individual involved. And yet, it's very difficult to address a particular doctrine without addressing the one who is proclaiming such doctrine, hence, Jesus naming the Pharisees, etc.

3. DO GOOD TO THEM WHO HATE YOU

This statement means, as is obvious, to return unkindness with kindness.

The story is told of a Chinese Christian who was working a plot of land under communist rule. His plot was immediately above the adjoining plot worked by another man, who was not a Christian, and who fervently avowed communistic atheism.

The Chinese Christian had gone to much labor and trouble to irrigate his plot of ground, which he had to do in order to secure the crop.

The unbeliever, who had his plot immediately below the plot worked by the Christian, went in during the night and made a breach in the mound of earth. This released all the water onto his land, thereby, watering it with a minimum of trouble, while causing the Christian to have to irrigate his all over again at the expense of much labor. Without saying anything, the Christian hauled the water by hand to his plot and irrigated it all over again. Besides that, he went in that night and performed some needed work on the unbeliever's plot.

The next morning, the unbeliever observed the situation and noted the work but didn't know how it was done.

That night, he carried out further damage to the Christian's plot, which necessitated more labor on the part of the believer. Again, nothing was said or done by the believer to the unbeliever, but he instead went in and worked several hours on the unbeliever's plot, performing much more needed work.

This went on for quite some time, with kindness being extended each and every time on the part of the believer for every act of unkindness on the part of the unbeliever.

It took several weeks. During this time, not a word was exchanged between them, but finally, the unbeliever came to the Christian and said, "I have disavowed your Jesus, but seeing your actions in the face of my unkindness, I want to know your Christ." He went on to say, "Anything that can put such actions of kindness and love in one's heart should be strongly desired, and to be sure, I want what you have."

That is the general idea, but, regrettably, it is not too often carried out.

4. PRAY FOR THOSE WHO DESPITEFULLY USE YOU AND PERSECUTE YOU

To pray thusly is to come very near to the Spirit of Christ. One person said, "Such persons would have never had a particular place in my prayers but for the injuries they have done to me."

How should we pray for such a person?

We should pray that God would move upon them and show them His way of love. This will turn them around as nothing else will, that is, if they will allow Him to do so! Actually, prayer is the only real weapon that can be successfully used against any and all.

All of these things done in the true Spirit of Christ help the participant at least as much, if not more, than the intended offender.

The worst thing that can happen to a believer is for hate to get in his heart over real or imagined wrongs. Such poisons the system and causes sickness, as well as terrible discomfort. More importantly, it violates the Word of God. So, the idea that only the offender is being hurt is grossly in error.

A PERSONAL EXPERIENCE

As most know, our headquarters for Jimmy Swaggart Ministries is in Baton Rouge, Louisiana. There was a certain investigative reporter there who did not like us, to say the least, and did everything within his power to hurt us, even to destroy us. I'm not speaking of something that was only in the local sense, but it was also even over CNN, which went out to over 150 countries.

We were in a prayer meeting the morning after a particular telecast. In obedience to the Word of the Lord, I tried to pray for the man. Knowing that the Lord had said that we should pray for those who despitefully use us and persecute us, I was doing my best, but not too successfully.

I finally stopped and just said to the Lord, "You know my heart. I'm trying to pray for this man as You have stated, but to no avail. I really wouldn't care too much if an eighteen-wheeler caused him great problems."

As anyone and everyone ought to know, the Lord cannot be fooled. He knows what is in our hearts even far better than we do.

Then the Lord spoke to me, saying, "I want you to show him the mercy and the grace that I have shown you."

The moment the Lord said that to me, everything changed. I saw everything, including him, in a different light. There was actually a love that was developed in my heart for him as I began to seek the face of the Lord, asking the Lord to help the man. Now I could say it and really mean what I was saying.

Once I considered how good and gracious the Lord had been to me, it was not so hard at all to show this man the same mercy and grace that the Lord had extended unto me. That's been years ago, and even to this day, I have no ill-will toward him, wishing him well.

CHILDREN OF THE FATHER

"That you may be the children of your Father which is in heaven: for He makes His sun to rise on the evil and on the good, and sends rain on the just and on the unjust" (Mat. 5:45).

"That you may be the children of your Father which is in heaven," means as the Father does, so shall true sons do!

"For He makes His sun to rise on the evil and on the good," portrays the Lord sending good on both alike! While it is true that the Lord will ultimately send judgment if sin is not dealt with, still, even this is done in a corrective sense instead of for the sake of mere punishment.

"And sends rain on the just and on the unjust," is meant to emphasize that the Lord does good to both groups. Consequently, we are to do likewise, which the entirety of these passages emphasizes. The next verse explains the higher action of the true child of God versus the child of Satan.

PUBLICANS

"For if you love them who love you, what reward have you? do not even the publicans the same?" (Mat. 5:46).

Verse 46 is meant to proclaim the superiority of true Bible Christianity. The question, *"For if you love them who love you, what reward have you?"* is meant to proclaim the type of love the world has, which, in effect, says, "Scratch my back, and I'll scratch yours."

By asking the question, *"Do not even the publicans the same?"* Christ was saying that such spurious love can be had by anyone and, in fact, is shared by anyone. As a result, it is of precious little consequence!

Publicans were tax-gatherers. They were despised by the Jews, claiming they had sold out to the heathen, i.e., the Romans. So, any reference to being less than this class was the lowest thing that could be said of anyone religious. In other words, in Israel, a publican was the lowest form of human life, at least in the minds of their countrymen.

As we read these statements made by Christ, we must understand that our faith must be anchored in Christ and the Cross at all times. Only then can the Holy Spirit properly help us, and only then can we do what is required of us.

Every prophecy in the Bible streams in one way or the other toward the Cross, even as every blessing streams from the Cross.

The great question is, "Does the church understand this?"

The truth is, if the preacher is not preaching *"Jesus Christ and Him crucified,"* he's really not preaching the gospel (I Cor. 1:17; 2:2).

THE MANNER OF THE PUBLICANS

Respecting the collecting of taxes, at that time, Rome sold certain districts in Israel, as well as other countries, to the highest bidder. The winner of the bid was then allowed to collect taxes in that area and could keep all that he collected. The amount above what he had paid was pure profit.

In other words, if he paid $1 million for a certain district and was able to collect $1.5 million, he had profited himself half a million dollars.

In the collection of taxes, he was given great latitude and authority and was backed by Rome. Consequently, many, if not most, publicans grew very rich. They were considered by Israel to be renegade Jews, who, as stated, had sold out their country for the sake of money and were, in turn, greatly despised.

Wondrously enough, the man who wrote the book of Matthew had been a publican. While Israel looked down greatly on publicans, Jesus did not follow that course of action.

So, Jesus was saying that if we only love those who love us, we are no better than the publicans who were greatly despised by the Jews.

BRETHREN

"And if you salute your brethren only, what do you more than others? do not even the publicans so?" (Mat. 5:47).

In verse 46, Jesus touched those of like action, while in verse 47, He touched those in kind. There was a reason for this.

The various different parties in Israel at that time, such as the Pharisees, Sadducees, and Herodians, virtually hated each other. Also, almost all Jews hated the Samaritans, who they looked at as half-breeds and, therefore, not Jews.

So, in the phrase, *"And if you salute your brethren only,"* Jesus was addressing one of the basic problems and sins in Israel. Likewise, any and all who feel that only people in their church are saved fall into this category.

Christ was saying that if one's love does not rise any higher than that, he is no better than those considered to be the worst sinners and criminals in Israel, i.e., publicans. This must have hit the Pharisees and others of like ilk extremely hard.

MATURITY

"Be you therefore perfect, even as your Father which is in heaven is perfect" (Mat. 5:48).

The idea of verse 48 is not that one can attain perfection, *"Even as your Father which is in heaven,"* but that he will fully and completely attain to that measure of love to which he as a created being was intended to attain. In other words, it is God's standard of measurement that is to be used rather than man's.

The word *perfect,* as it applies to God, even though meaning "sinless perfection," does not refer to such in the life of the believer because such is impossible. However, a perfect God can command no less in His disciples, and to be sure, it is a state to which every believer must aspire, although continually falling short (Rom. 3:23).

The Mosaic law demanded perfection, although it was never attained in any individual, even Moses, but only in Christ. As a result, faith in Christ, as the representative man, makes one a participant of the perfect walk of Christ.

So, in the mind of God, the acceptance of Christ, who is perfect, gives one Christ's perfection. It is all done by faith, as it can only be done by faith; however, it must be faith in Christ and His Cross as the complete object.

Take the name of Jesus with you,
Child of sorrow and of woe;
It will joy and comfort give you,
Take it then, wherever you go.

Take the name of Jesus ever,
As a shield from every snare.
If temptations round you gather,
Breathe that holy name in prayer.

Oh the precious name of Jesus,
How it thrills our souls with joy,
When His loving arms receive us,
And His songs our tongues employ!

At the name of Jesus bowing,
Falling prostrate at His feet,
King of kings in heaven we'll crown Him,
When our journey is complete.

THE SERMON *on the* MOUNT

CHAPTER 4

RELATIONSHIP WITH GOD

RELATIONSHIP WITH GOD

"TAKE HEED THAT YOU do not your alms before men, to be seen of them: otherwise you have no reward of your Father who is in heaven" (Mat. 6:1).

APPROVAL FROM HEAVEN

In the previous chapter, we discussed how the Lord deals with issues of the heart. This chapter focuses on how He deals with relationship. His teaching concerns itself with the most basic fundamentals of righteous living, but yet, that which forms the foundation of our relationship with God.

"Take heed that you do not your alms before men, to be seen of them," strikes at the very heart of our reason for giving.

Why do we give to God?

In beginning this phrase with the words, *"Take heed,"* the Lord is proclaiming the seriousness of the matter as it is seen by God.

Sadly, many people give to get, while others give, as here stated, to be seen. Paul said we should give to God *"to prove the sincerity of your love"* (II Cor. 8:8).

Once again, if our faith is exclusively in Christ and the Cross, our giving will be as it should be.

If any doctrine in the Bible is given preeminence over the foundation, which is the Cross, the priority then becomes wrong, and the end results will never be good. The only way that the sinner can be saved is to have faith in Christ and what He did at the Cross on our behalf. That is the very heart of redemption. While the believing sinner may not, and, in fact, doesn't, understand anything about the Cross, still, that is the only means of his redemption.

Likewise, the only way a Christian can live a victorious, overcoming life is by having constant faith in the Cross of Christ. This means that he looks to the finished work of Christ constantly for all things, understanding that Jesus paid it all.

THE REWARD

"Otherwise you have no reward of your Father who is in heaven," means that many believers, if not most, will not be rewarded by the Lord for their giving. In truth, it is not even looked at by the Lord as giving. If it is given in the wrong spirit and attitude, it is counted by the Lord as nothing at all! Read again verse 1.

If these stipulations are to be followed, as they certainly must be, this means that only a tiny percentage of money given to that which purports to be of God is actually recognized by Him as such. Let's look at that which God will not honor or recognize as true giving to His work.

Giving to that which is a lie or a sham—no matter how much the lie is believed—is not honored by God as true giving, which ought to be obvious. The believer should have more discernment than that.

A PERSONAL EXPERIENCE

Sometime back, I looked at a structure that was built at a cost of between $10 and $20 million, which wasn't used at all, and for all basic purposes, was sitting empty. And yet, tens of thousands of people had given sums of money to build this structure because they were told the work carried on within its confines would facilitate the taking of the gospel to the world. To be frank, that which was supposed to be done in this building, and for which the people had given their money, to my knowledge, has never been done at all. In fact, absolutely nothing has ever been done with the building.

It was a money-raising ploy, pure and simple, and it succeeded very well. Without a doubt, two or three times the amount needed was actually raised, with virtually all of it being wasted. Regrettably, hundreds of millions of dollars each year, if not more, go into such grandiose projects, which serve no purpose at all but are merely fund-raising schemes that are believed by the people to be a genuine work of God. As stated, true Christians should have better discernment, but sadly, there aren't many true Christians!

Irrespective as to how sincere people may be in the giving of money to such projects, still, it is a scam, pure and simple, and cannot be honored by God. It is simply a bad investment regarding that which proposes to be the work of God but, in reality, isn't.

FALSE DOCTRINE

Money given to propagate false doctrine certainly cannot be concluded as one truly giving to the work of God. In effect, all erroneous doctrines are initially instigated by demon spirits. Consequently, no matter how sincere the individuals may be in their giving to such error, still, it is not of God and cannot be blessed by God. In effect, such giving aids and abets the work of Satan. Tragically, this includes the far greater majority of that which is labeled "Christian."

This does not mean that all true, godly preachers have all the light on all biblical subjects, for such certainly is not the case. However, we are speaking of obvious false doctrine that is contrary to Scripture and is error, plain and simple, no matter how sincerely believed.

THE APOSTLE PAUL

Let's use Paul as an example. As is known, Paul planted churches over Asia Minor and even into Greece, which is in Europe. After he would leave and go into other fields of endeavor, Judaizers would come from Jerusalem and Judaea into his churches, seeking to get Gentiles to start keeping the law of Moses, etc.

Judaizers were Jews who claimed to believe in Christ, but at the same time, claimed that one had to keep the law in order to be a complete Christian. Some even claimed that to be saved one had to keep the law of Moses (Acts 15:1).

Pure and simple, this was false doctrine. And yet, there were people in these churches, people who had been saved under the ministry of Paul, who were being duped into believing this error and even giving money to these individuals, whomever they may have been.

Now, I'm sure that one could not seriously think that God would bless such giving, which, in actuality, was hurting, if not destroying, the gospel of grace.

No, the Lord could not bless such that was tearing down His kingdom, and neither can He bless such presently. Unfortunately, most are going in that direction.

SATAN'S MINISTERS

The following is what the Holy Spirit through Paul said of false teachers, and I'm going to take it directly from The Expositor's Study Bible, including the notes:

> But what I do, that I will do (I will continue to pursue the course of life I have been pursuing), that I may cut off occasion from them which desire occasion (he will not do anything that will give his enemies occasion to find fault, at least, truthfully); that wherein they glory (they claim to not be interested in your money, but that's not true), they may be found even

as we. (If they aren't interested in your money, let them conduct themselves as we do and not take your money.) *For such are false apostles, deceitful workers* (they have no rightful claim to the apostolic office; they are deceivers), *transforming themselves into the apostles of Christ.* (They have called themselves to this office.) *And no marvel* (true believers should not be surprised); *for Satan himself is transformed into an angel of light.* (This means he pretends to be that which he is not.) *Therefore it is no great thing if his ministers* (Satan's ministers) *also be transformed as the ministers of righteousness* (despite their claims, they were 'Satan's ministers' because they preached something other than the Cross [1 Cor. 1:17-18, 21, 23; 2:2; Gal. 1:8-9]); *whose end shall be according to their works* (that 'end' is spiritual destruction [Phil. 3:18-19]) (II Cor. 11:12-15).

GREED

Believers are to expect the Lord to bless their giving. His Word plainly says so. In fact, the only manner in which the Lord approves of us proving Him is in our giving. He stated: *"Bring you all the tithes into the storehouse, that there may be meat in My house, and prove Me now herewith, says the Lord of Hosts, if I will not open you the windows of heaven, and pour you out a blessing, that there shall not be room enough to receive it"* (Mal. 3:10).

Please allow me once again to quote the notes from The Expositor's Study Bible regarding verse 10:

'*Bring you all the tithes into the storehouse,*' referred to the temple and cities of the Levites under the old covenant. Under the new covenant, it refers to the place where one's soul is fed, wherever that might be. Some have claimed that the local church is the 'storehouse' where all giving is to be brought; however, that is incorrect, inasmuch as those who propose such fail to understand what 'church' actually is! 'Church' is made up of all members of the body of Christ, irrespective of who they are or where they are. It has nothing to do with the building, organization, or religious institution. It is the 'message' which must be supported—not an institution. The phrase, '*That there may be meat in My house,*' has reference to the support of the priesthood in the temple of old. The Lord has no such 'house' at present because Jesus fulfilled all that the ancient temple represented, with Him now residing through the agency of the Holy Spirit in the hearts and lives of all believers [I Cor. 3:16]. (In other words, every believer constitutes His house.)

PROVING GOD

'*And prove Me now herewith, says the Lord of Hosts,*' presents a challenge presented by the Lord for men to prove Him regarding the rewards of tithing. '*If I will not open you the windows of heaven, and pour you out a blessing, that there shall not be room enough to receive it,*' speaks of a superabundant amount. The same phrase, 'windows of heaven,' is used in Genesis 7:11 regarding the flood; therefore, we are speaking of blessings unparalleled!

People should expect the Lord to bless their giving. They should expect Him to open the windows of heaven exactly as He said that He would. Believers should expect Him to bless constantly, that is, if we properly obey Him. It's not that we earn the blessings, for the Lord has nothing for sale. It's that we function in the realm of obedience.

God has chosen tithes and offerings to support His work. He could have done it in a thousand other ways had He so desired, but He chose this method.

Why?

He did it this way in order to bless us. We give to Him, and He gives back to us in one way or the other *"good measure, pressed down, and shaken together, and running over"* (Lk. 6:38).

THE CROSS OF CHRIST AND PROSPERITY

We teach from the Bible that every single blessing that comes to the child of God has Christ as its source and the Cross as its means. I mean every blessing. This means that the Cross of Christ must be the object of our faith, which then gives the Holy Spirit liberty to work in our lives (Rom. 6:1-14; 8:1-11; I Cor. 1:17-18, 23; 2:2; Col. 2:10-15).

In other words, if the believer needs an increase in pay, there is an increase in pay in the Cross. If the believer needs a better car, there's a better car in the Cross. If the believer needs a better house, there's a better house in the Cross. If the believer needs healing, there is healing in the Cross. If the believer needs deliverance, there is deliverance in the Cross. Most definitely, the major purpose and reason for the Cross of Christ was and is the redemption of humanity. Everything else takes second place. Nevertheless, there is room at the Cross for every single need that we have. To be sure, Jesus paid it all.

THE OLD TESTAMENT AND THE NEW TESTAMENT

Some argue that the great passage in Malachi that we've just quoted was only for believers in Old Testament times. It most definitely was for them, but it is even greater for us. Paul said:

But now (since the Cross) *as He* (the Lord Jesus) *obtained a more excellent ministry* (the new covenant in Jesus' blood is superior and takes the place of the old covenant in animal blood), *by how much also He is the mediator of a better covenant* (proclaims the fact that Christ officiates between God and man according to the arrangements of the new covenant), *which was established upon better promises.* (This presents the new covenant explicitly based on the cleansing and forgiveness of all sin, which the old covenant could not do.) *For if that first covenant had been faultless* (proclaims the fact that the first covenant was definitely not faultless; as stated, it was based on animal blood, which was vastly inferior to the precious blood of Christ), *then should no place have been sought for the second* (proclaims the necessity of the second covenant) (Heb. 8:6-7) (The Expositor's Study Bible).

THE NEW COVENANT

In effect, Jesus is the new covenant. This means that He does not merely have the new covenant or properly understand the new covenant but, in reality, *is* the new covenant. As God is love, Jesus Christ is the new covenant.

Concerning the new covenant, the Holy Spirit through the apostle Paul made the following statements:

- The new covenant is a *"more excellent ministry"* (Heb. 8:6).

- It is *"established upon better promises"* (Heb. 8:6).

- The first covenant was faulty, while the new covenant has no fault whatsoever because it's all in Christ (Heb. 8:7).

Now, all of this tells me that whatever was promised under the old covenant can be had in triplicate under the new covenant because in today's modern vernacular, we now have a much better contract.

MONEY MUST NEVER BE THE OBJECT

Unfortunately, a great part of the modern church has things other than righteousness and holiness as its goal.

However, let me warn you, if our motives are centered on money, we then forfeit the blessing, despite the fact that God most definitely gloriously blesses His people. We must never forget that.

While every believer wants and desires blessings from the Lord, and rightly so, still, everything must be put in its proper order. Considering the great price that Jesus has paid, the Holy Spirit did not bring us to Christ for the sole purpose of our being financially rich. He brought us to Christ that we might be made into the image of Christ, that righteousness and holiness may be the staples of our life and living. I'll warn you that at the moment that ceases to be preeminent, the blessings stop; however, as long as our emphasis is on Christ and Christ alone, the blessings will always follow.

REWARD?

"Therefore when you do your alms, do not sound a trumpet before you, as the hypocrites do in the synagogues and in the streets, that they may have glory of men. Verily I say unto you, they have their reward" (Mat. 6:2).

The phrase, *"Therefore when you do your alms,"* proclaims the necessity of giving, and in whatever capacity. Now the Lord tells us what not to do:

- *"Do not sound a trumpet before you"*: the idea was taken from the Pharisees, who, for the most part, made a great show of their giving so that all would know exactly from whom it came and how much was given, especially if it was a sum of notable size.

- Consequently, that which was being done was but for
  one purpose—to be seen of men.

- *"As the hypocrites do in the synagogues and in the streets"*:
  Therefore, Jesus labels all who do such things as hypocrites.
  The word *hypocrite* refers to an actor who plays a part but is
  really not the part. In other words, it was only *play acting.*

- *"That they may have glory of men"*: regrettably, so much
  of that which purports to be the work of God is done
  for this very purpose.

- *"They have their reward"*: consequently, don't expect anything from God because what is done is not true giving,
  at least in the sense that He will reward.

GLORY FROM MEN

*"But when you do alms, let not your left hand know what your
right hand does"* (Mat. 6:3).

Many Christians, if not most, try to be holy and righteous
by trusting in good works instead of having faith totally in what
Christ did at the Cross. Such an attitude only breeds self-righteousness, which plagues the modern church to a disastrous
degree. When Christians sin and then try to overcome the
problem through a series of laws and rules, which only tend to
compound the situation instead of solve the problem, the problem is made worse. The Cross of Christ alone addresses men.

Many people have attempted to take verse 3 literally, completely missing the intent and purpose of what Christ was saying. The idea is simply that one is not to give to receive glory from men.

THE METHOD

For instance, many times in church services, the Holy Spirit will move upon individuals to give certain amounts of money and to make public what they are giving. At times, such is used by the Holy Spirit, which encourages others to give, and it builds faith.

While it certainly may be true that some people, even in these Holy Spirit-inspired circumstances, may be giving for self-glory, still, that is a problem with their own hearts and not with the method. In other words, the method is not wrong, only the heart of the individual.

As well, some have attempted to twist this Scripture to make it mean that anyone who gives publicly is violating this Scripture and, consequently, violating the commands of Christ.

To do so is to judge in a negative way the motives of every single individual who is giving, which, within itself, violates the words of Christ to *"judge not"* (Mat. 7:1).

Jesus was not teaching that the giving of these individuals was wrong, or not even necessarily that the method in which they chose to give was wrong. Instead, He was teaching that the purpose of their hearts was wrong because they desired to receive glory from men. That is what Christ was opposing.

SECRET

"That your alms may be in secret: and your Father who sees in secret Himself shall reward you openly" (Mat. 6:4).

The phrase, *"That your alms may be in secret,"* simply means that from the heart, it is done as unto the Lord. This would go not only for the giving of money but any and all work, labor, service, and effort expended for the cause of Christ. It must not be done for show, but instead, for the Lord's eyes only.

"And Your Father who sees in secret Himself," refers to the Lord alone, who is to guide and direct one's actions, because the person and all his goods actually belong to the Lord.

In this manner, the Spirit guides the destiny of all, while in the manner opposed by Christ, such is guided by the flesh, which can never be accepted by God (Rom. 8:8).

"Shall reward you openly," refers to what the Lord will do if we abide by His Word.

In other words, one can be rewarded by man or God, but not by both! If one wants the glory of men, one cannot have the glory of God. Conversely, if one has the glory of God, he will not have the glory of men.

PRAYER

"And when you pray, you shall not be as the hypocrites are: for they love to pray standing in the synagogues and in the corners of the streets, that they may be seen of men. Verily I say unto you, They have their reward" (Mat. 6:5).

As the Lord dealt with giving, which is very important in His sight and most definitely should be in ours, as well, He now deals with prayer, which is, likewise, of supreme significance. In these passages we learn that those who make God's interest their own are assured that He will make their interest His own.

"And when you pray," assumes that Christians, in fact, pray! Tragically, in the modern church, it would probably be better stated, "And if you pray." Prayer is the most powerful force in which a believer can engage, that is, if it is truly done in humility and is done scripturally. Shortly, the Lord would give the model prayer, which, as we shall see, would embody the very attitude and spiritual posture for which all should strive.

It is my contention that the believer cannot really have a proper prayer life without first understanding the Cross of Christ as it concerns our daily living.

The entirety of our union with Christ is predicated solely upon faith, and it must be faith in Christ and what Christ has done for us at the Cross (I Cor. 1:17). The only faith recognized by the Holy Spirit is that which has as its object the Cross of Christ.

The Holy Spirit only asks of us that we exhibit faith in the Cross of Christ and understand that it was there that all victory was won, and we mean all victory!

HYPOCRITES

The phrase, *"You shall not be as the hypocrites are,"* was by and large referring to the Pharisees.

The phrases, *"Standing in the synagogues"* and *"in the corners of the street,"* did not mean that it was wrong to pray there, but instead, that the Pharisees' love of praise made them choose these places specifically *"that they may be seen of men."* To be sure, such is a waste of time and is the very opposite of the truly humble heart.

It is strange that while in the world, the "flesh" doesn't want anyone to know that it has any thoughts of God; however, once it gets in the church, the same *flesh* desires that all know, see, and understand just how much their thoughts are on God. Consequently, the flesh in the Christian is far more deadly than in the unbeliever.

"Verily I say unto you, They have their reward," proclaims the foolishness of such action and the fact that God does not hear such prayers, at least to answer them, and, therefore, they are in vain.

WHAT IS THE FLESH?

As Paul used the word over and over again (Rom., Chpt. 8), it refers to that which is indicative to human beings. I speak of talent, education, ability, intellect, motivation, etc.

Those things within themselves aren't necessarily wrong; however, they become wrong when we try to use them as our sole means of living this life for the Lord. It simply cannot be done that way. That's the reason that the Holy Spirit through Paul said, *"So then they who are in the flesh cannot please God"* (Rom. 8:8).

The way of the child of God is faith in Christ and the Cross, and faith in Christ and the Cross exclusively. Then the Holy Spirit, who works totally and completely within the confines, so to speak, of the finished work of Christ, will help us mightily. Otherwise, we greatly limit Him. I speak of trying to do what we cannot do in the first place, and for which Jesus paid such a price. It is so much easier to do it His way than to try to do it our way, which, in fact, cannot be done.

At the fall, man was greatly weakened, and to be sure, the clinging vines of the fall still affect the child of God. Without fail, we must place our faith and our energy, so to speak, in Christ and what Christ has done for us at the Cross. Only then will the Holy Spirit work on our behalf as He desires to do (Rom. 8:10).

If one thinks we speak of the Cross too much, then that automatically says that such a person does not really understand the Cross. If he understood it, at least as the Word of God gives it to us, he would not be complaining and asking for less, but would rather be asking for more.

WHEN YOU PRAY

"But you, when you pray, enter into your closet, and when you have shut your door, pray to your Father who is in secret; and your Father who sees in secret shall reward you openly" (Mat. 6:6).

"But you, when you pray," now refers to the true manner of prayer and that which God will honor and reward.

"Enter into your closet, and when you have shut your door," refers to secrecy and privacy respecting communion with the Lord,

whether petitions asked or consecration requested. It does not mean that one is to literally enter into a closet or pray alone, but it simply means that our praying must not be to be heard of men, but rather of God.

We must understand that the entirety of our union with Christ is predicated solely upon faith. However, if it is faith that God will recognize, it must be faith in Christ and His finished work. To claim that we have faith in the Word while ignoring the Cross presents, in a sense, *"another Jesus"* (II Cor. 11:4). The Christian can only be holy and righteous by trusting in the righteousness of God, which is freely given upon faith in the finished work of Christ.

PRAYER TO OUR HEAVENLY FATHER

The phrase, *"Pray to your Father who is in secret,"* has reference to a very personal communion between the Lord and the believer.

My grandmother taught me to have a prayer life, which commenced when I was 8 years old and has continued unto this day some 75 years later.

Each morning, I go to the office just before our telecast begins at 7 a.m. central time, and I spend at least 20 minutes with the Lord. This is a must because His help is so very much needed for what we are doing. I have to have guidance, direction, and empowerment, which He so freely gives.

Every evening when I go home, I spend another 20 minutes or so with the Lord in prayer, thanking Him for the day and once again seeking His guidance and direction.

Most of my praying is made up of thanksgiving to the Lord for His goodness, mercy, and grace. As well, almost every time that the Lord has spoken to my heart about very important things, it has been during times of prayer. In fact, I cannot see how that a Christian can have any type of relationship with the Lord without having a prayer life. The times I spend with Him are not long periods, as stated, normally about 20 minutes, but they are very special to me.

This I believe: If every believer would place his or her faith exclusively in Christ and what Christ has done for us at the Cross and maintain it thusly, and, as well, would set aside a prayer time each day—and I mean seven days a week without fail—they would find everything about their lives beginning to improve. Such believers would find their lives dramatically changed for the better and, above all, their lives would continue to get better.

OPEN REWARD

"And your Father who sees in secret shall reward you openly," refers to a secret petition (at least at times) receiving a public answer.

As well, in this Scripture we are plainly told that the Lord will answer prayer. Isn't that beautiful? Isn't that wonderful? To be able to tell the Lord our needs and to know that He in His way is going to meet these needs is wonderful indeed. He plainly stated, *"And your Father who sees in secret shall reward you openly."* Do you believe that?

I have believed it all of my life, and I have seen Him work miracle after miracle, and I am expecting that the greatest is yet to come.

VAIN REPETITION

"But when you pray, use not vain repetitions, as the heathen do: for they think that they shall be heard for their much speaking" (Mat. 6:7).

"But when you pray, use not vain repetitions," speaks to the practice of the Hindus, Roman Catholics, and others who believe that by repeating the same prayer hundreds of times, *"they shall be heard for their much speaking."*

Regrettably, the Jews at that time, and especially the Pharisees, were coming perilously close to the heathen by their use of certain phrases over and over again, which constituted *"vain repetitions."*

Such is not a prayer from the heart, but is rather a formula or doing something by rote, in which the individual seems to think that the act itself carries some type of spiritual power. The Muslims pray five times a day; however, it is not prayer heard by God as is here plainly stated!

The Lord uses the words, *"they think,"* respecting their being heard, which, in effect, says, as well, that they are not heard!

THE HEAVENLY FATHER

"Do not be like unto them: for your Father knows what things you have need of, before you ask Him" (Mat. 6:8).

The finished work of Christ has as much to do with our everyday walk before the Lord as it did our initial salvation experience. That's one of the reasons Christians run all over the world, chasing one fad after the other. They don't know anything about the application of the Cross within their lives on a daily basis. Therefore, they walk in defeat. Jesus never really said anything about preachers delivering people, at least as we think of such. He did say that we are to *"preach deliverance to the captives,"* which refers to preaching the Cross (Lk. 4:18; I Cor. 1:18).

DO NOT BE LIKE UNTO THEM

This means that we are to pray as the Lord here tells us to pray and not like the heathen. True prayer to the Lord is not the easiest task there is. Satan opposes it in every way possible. Therefore, when we pray, we surely should obey the Lord, which will guarantee that our prayers be heard. To do otherwise is a fruitless exercise! In fact, in this dialogue on prayer, the Lord will tell us step by step how to pray.

THE LORD KNOWS WHAT WE NEED

This phrase is meant to extol the omniscience of God. He knows all things—past, present, and future—irrespective of what they might be, and He does not have to be stirred to action by vain repetition. Actually, many godly people pray and say very little, at least as far as the mouth is concerned; however, what little is said comes from the heart and is greatly honored by God.

BEFORE WE ASK HIM

The entire sentence is, *"For your Father knows what things you have need of, before you ask Him."*

As stated, this pertains to the omniscience of God, which means, as we've already stated, that He knows all things, past, present, and future. So, the idea is that we should realize that God is not lacking in knowledge and that we have to remind Him of what is needed. Actually, and as plainly stated, He already knows.

Consequently, many would ask if, in fact, that is the case, why should we need to pray at all.

Prayer is not just petition. It includes worship, communion, fellowship, and consecration. It involves far more than just asking the Lord for something.

In truth, many times the believer will pray for long periods of time and ask the Lord for very little if anything! The time will be spent in worshiping the Lord, which He justly deserves and which strengthens us greatly.

That should not seem so strange. The ties between a parent and his child are strengthened greatly when the child tenderly and kindly tells the parent how much he is loved.

THE PERSON OF GOD

God is a person; He is not a machine. As such, He has feelings exactly as we have, although to a different degree. As such, He wants communion between His children and Himself.

While prayer is not the only way such can be done, still, it is a way and, without a doubt, is one of the most important ways. As well, He desires that we *"ask Him"* respecting our petitions, irrespective of His total knowledge. Such builds faith, trust, and responsibility.

As we've already stated, prayer carries with it such rewards that we ought to have a prayer life that is constant. Please believe me, this is the most rewarding experience that one could ever begin to have. How so happy I am that my grandmother taught me to pray. She taught me to believe God. In fact, she told me many times, "Jimmy, God is a big God, so ask big." I have never forgotten that, and it has helped me to touch this world for Christ.

THE LORD'S PRAYER

"After this manner therefore you should pray: Our Father who is in heaven, hallowed be Your name. Your kingdom come, Your will be done in earth, as it is in heaven. Give us this day our daily bread. And forgive us our debts, as we forgive our debtors. And lead us not into temptation, but deliver us from evil: for Yours is the kingdom, and the power, and the glory, forever. Amen" (Mat. 6:9-13).

Now we come to that which is commonly referred to as the Lord's Prayer. It contains seven petitions—three respecting God and four respecting man. Those respecting God come first.

This prayer is also recorded in Luke, although in a slightly shorter version; consequently, controversy has raged as to the original version.

Inasmuch as Matthew was written first, no doubt, the Holy Spirit superintended the entirety of the version in this gospel with a slightly abbreviated form in Luke's gospel.

The phrase, *"After this manner therefore you should pray,"* is meant to be in total contrast to the heathen practice.

As well, in picking up on the previous verse, it is to be prayed in full confidence that the Father will hear and answer according to His will. In fact, the believer most definitely should want nothing but the perfect will of God in all things.

As we go into this extremely important explanation by our Lord, we should understand always that it is the Cross of Christ that makes possible all salvation, all deliverance, and all victory.

Regrettably, the world ever since has been trying to make a new god other than the Lord of the Bible, while the church has been trying to make another sacrifice other than the Cross of Christ. Both lead to destruction.

OUR FATHER WHO IS IN HEAVEN

The first two words, *"Our Father,"* destroy the doctrine of a false humility that teaches that in prayer, the supplicant should take up a position as far from God as possible and address Him by many august titles.

Then, according to that teaching, only after a very lengthened prayer, the term *Father* may be used. Finally, the teaching states that even then, it must be used with much timidity. However, to be timid when God commands boldness is to be disobedient (Heb. 4:16).

God is my Father by virtue of my being born again. As a result of this all-important experience, Paul said:

For you have not received the spirit of bondage (to try to live after a system of works and laws will only succeed in placing one in 'bondage') *again to fear* (such living creates a perpetual climate of fear in the heart of such a believer); *but you have received the Spirit of adoption* (the Holy Spirit has adopted us into the family of God), *whereby we cry, Abba, Father* (the Holy Spirit enables the child of God to call God 'Father,' which is done so because of Jesus Christ).

CHILDREN OF GOD

The Spirit itself (Himself) *bears witness with our spirit* (means that He is constantly speaking and witnessing certain things to us), *that we are the children of God* (means that we are such now and should enjoy all the privileges of such; we can do so if we will understand that all these privileges come to us from God by the means of the Cross):

JOINT-HEIRS

And if children (children of God), *then heirs* (a privilege); *heirs of God* (the highest enrichment of all), *and joint-heirs with Christ* (everything that belongs to Christ belongs to us through the Cross, which was done for us); *if so be that we suffer with Him* (doesn't pertain to mere suffering, but rather suffering 'with Him,' referring to His suffering at the Cross, which brought us total victory), *that we may be also glorified together* (He has been glorified, and we shall be glorified; all made possible by the Cross) (Rom. 8:15-17) (The Expositor's Study Bible).

THE JEWS

For Jesus to address Jehovah as *"Father"* and to instruct His followers to do so was completely revolutionary to the Jews. In their false humility, they would never have assumed such familiarity.

The main reason was that few really knew Him! Therefore, only His children can address Him accordingly.

THE FATHERHOOD OF GOD AND
THE BROTHERHOOD OF MAN

As well, this in no way promotes the unscriptural doctrine of the "Fatherhood of God, and the brotherhood of man," which teaches that God is the Father of all and that all men are brothers. While God is the Creator of all, that is as far as it goes. God becomes the Father of the individual when that person is born again.

To say it another way: God is the Father only of those who have accepted Him as Lord and Saviour and, consequently, have become His children. Otherwise, all men are *"sons of Adam"* and not *"sons of God,"* which means to be born again (Gen. 5:3).

THE SPIRIT BODY OF GOD

Even though God is everywhere and, therefore, omnipresent, still, His Spirit body occupies His throne in heaven.

One of the visions of Daniel proclaims that which we have stated. It says:

> I saw in the night visions, and, behold, One like the Son of Man came with the clouds of heaven, and came to the Ancient of Days, and they brought Him near before Him. And there was given Him dominion, and glory, and a kingdom, that all people, nations, and languages, should serve Him: His dominion is an everlasting dominion, which shall not pass away, and His kingdom that which shall not be destroyed (Dan. 7:13-14).

The "Son of Man" is God the Son, the Lord Jesus Christ, while the "Ancient of Days" is God the Father. The Holy Spirit inspired this, so that makes up the Trinity.

JOHN THE BELOVED

John, as well, gave us another glimpse of the throne of God, which, in effect, portrays the Trinity.

John said, "And immediately I was in the Spirit: and, behold, a throne was set in heaven, and One sat on the throne (this was God the Father). And He who sat was to look upon like a jasper and a sardine stone: and there was a rainbow round about the throne, in sight like unto an emerald" (Rev. 4:2-3)

As John had seen the throne of God and, as well, God Himself, he now saw the Lord Jesus Christ symbolized as *"a Lamb as it had been slain"* (Rev. 5:6). Of course, this symbolized the Cross of Christ. Then he spoke of the *"seven Spirits of God sent forth into all the earth"* (Rev. 5:6). We know there aren't seven Holy Spirit's of God but only one Holy Spirit, with His seven attributes enumerated (Isa. 11:2). Then John said, *"And He* (this was the Lord Jesus Christ) *came and took the book out of the right hand of Him* (this is God the Father) *who sat upon the throne"* (Rev. 5:7).

GOD HAS A SPIRIT BODY

Some people object to the statement that God has a Spirit body. We know He does not have a flesh, blood, and bone body, even though the Scripture mentions Him having a head, hands, eyes, etc., therefore, we must conclude that He has some type of Spirit body (Job 11:5; Dan. 7:9; Rev. 4:2-3).

As well, heaven is a place and not just the endless stretch of the universe, etc.

All the statements in the Bible concerning God the Father recognize Him to be a person and not some invisible nothingness floating around somewhere, filling all matter and space.

Even though the Bible teaches the omnipresence of God, it does not teach the omni-body of God, in other words, that His body (Spirit body) is in many different places at the same time.

When God appeared to Abraham in His Spirit body, even though His presence was still in heaven as well as everywhere else, still, His Spirit body was in front of Abraham and, at least at that time, no place else (Gen. 18:1).

ANTHROPOMORPHISMS

Some object to these statements, claiming that such descriptions as given by the Bible regarding the bodily appearances of God, plus body parts such as *"eyes, ears, hands,"* etc., are but anthropomorphic, meaning "human parts ascribed to God, which He really does not have, but given so that we may understand Him better."

If that is true, that puts the Holy Spirit, who superintended the writing of the Bible, in the position of encouraging lies. Of course, we know that is untrue! Therefore, why not simply believe what the Bible says about God, which means to *"rightly divide the word of truth."* This means, among other things, to compare Scripture with Scripture. The Bible never contradicts itself, and neither does it say that things are when they really aren't!

So, when people pray to God the Father as they should (Jn. 16:23), they are not praying to some disembodied spirit floating around in space. Instead, they are praying to a person with attributes, feelings, passions, likes, and desires, but yet, One who is omniscient (all-knowing), omnipotent (all-powerful), and omnipresent (everywhere).

As well, God is uncaused, unformed, unmade, uncreated, and has always been, always is, and always shall be (Isa. 40:12-15; 45:5-7).

HALLOWED BE YOUR NAME

After addressing the heavenly Father, immediately the praise and worship begins.

Here we are told how important the name of God actually is. He went under many names in the Old Testament in order to express His personality, and above all that, what He meant to be to His people. The following are some of His names:

- **Elohim.** This is the plural of "Eloah" and means "Gods." This name indicates the relation of God to man as creator and is in contrast with *"Jehovah,"* which indicates Him in covenant relationship with creation. As well, it speaks of Him as an object of worship (Gen. 1:1; 2:3). This name is used 2,701 times in the Old Testament.

- **Yehovah.** (Jehovah): This name is used 6,437 times in the Old Testament and means "the self-existent or eternal One—Lord." It was the Jewish national name of God. Where translated "God," it is used with another name, *"Adonai, LORD—Adonai-Jehovah, LORD God"* (Gen. 15:2, 8; Deut. 3:24; 9:26; Josh. 7:7).

- **El.** This means "strength." "El" is the strong and mighty one; the Almighty; the Most High God (Gen. 14:18-22; 16:13; 17:1). This is used 220 times in the Old Testament.

- **Eloah.** This means "deity; God, the Divine One" (Deut. 32:15, 17; II Chron. 32:15; Neh. 9:17). This name is used 56 times in the Old Testament.

- **Elah.** This simply means "God" (Ezra 4:24; 5:1-17; 6:3-18; 7:12-27; Dan. 2:11-47).

- **Tsur.** This means "rock" or "refuge" (Isa. 44:8).

- **Theos.** This is the main Greek word for "God" in the New Testament and means "Deity; the Supreme God" (Mat. 1:23; 3:9, 16; 4:3-10). As well, this word Theos is used in various combinations.

- **Jehovah-Jireh.** The Lord will provide (Gen. 22:8-14).

- **Jehovah-Nissi.** The Lord our banner (Ex. 17:15).

- **Jehovah-Ropheka.** The Lord our healer (Ex. 15:26).

- **Jehovah-Shalom.** The Lord our peace (Jud. 6:24).

- **Jehovah-Tsidkeenu.** The Lord our righteousness (Jer. 23:6; 33:16).

- **Jehovah-Mekaddishkem.** The Lord our sanctifier (Ex. 31:13; Lev. 20:8; 21:8).

- **Jehovah-Saboath.** The Lord of Hosts (I Sam. 1:3).

- **Jehovah-Shammah.** The Lord is present (Ezek. 48:35).

- **Jehovah-Elyon.** The Lord Most High (Ps. 7:17; 47:2; 97:9).

- **Jehovah-Rohi.** The Lord my shepherd (Ps. 23:1).

- **Jehovah-Hoseenu.** The Lord our maker (Ps. 95:6).

- **Jehovah-Eloheenu.** The Lord our God (Ps. 99:5, 8-9).

- **Jehovah-Eloheka.** The Lord your God (Ex. 20:2, 5, 7).

- **Jehovah-Elohay.** The Lord my God (Zech. 14:5).

- **Jesus.** His name given in the incarnation, and it means "Saviour."

SAVIOUR

Of all the names of the Lord in the Old Testament under which God expressed Himself, all were designed but for one purpose, and that was to lead up to His name as Saviour. That was His purpose from the very beginning—to redeem mankind. As well, it could only be done under the name "Jesus" (Joshua in the Hebrew).

As such, we worship Him, and in actuality, worship Him through His name, which more than anything else, expresses who He is and what He has done for us.

FANNY CROSBY

Fanny Crosby wrote the following song many years ago:

To God be the glory, great things He has done,
So loved He the world that He gave us His Son,
Who yielded His life an atonement for sin,
And opened the Life Gate that all may go in.

Oh perfect redemption, the purchase of blood!
To every believer the promise of God;
The vilest offender who truly believes,
That moment from Jesus a pardon receives.

Great things He has taught us,
Great things He has done,
And great our rejoicing through Jesus the Son;
But purer, and higher, and greater will be,
Our wonder, our transport, when Jesus we see.

Praise the Lord, praise the Lord,
Let the earth hear His voice!
Praise the Lord, praise the Lord,
Let the people rejoice!
Oh come to the Father through Jesus the Son,
And give Him the glory,
Great things He has done.

YOUR KINGDOM COME

After offering the Lord praise and worship, which should begin our supplication before Him, especially considering that the psalmist also said, *"Enter into His gates with thanksgiving, and into His courts with praise"* (Ps. 100:4), our next concern should be for the entrance of the kingdom of God on earth. The suffering and heartache that have invaded this world due to Satan and the fall of man must be healed.

As far as is known, God's kingdom now reigns supreme throughout His entire creation, with the exception of Satan, the fallen angels, and planet earth. Jesus came that this might be rectified, and, to be sure, it ultimately will be.

THE KINGDOM OF GOD

The coming of the kingdom of God to this earth will dispel all sin, wickedness, and iniquity that cause all heartache, pain, sickness, suffering, and death. When His kingdom is firmly established, which it soon shall be, then *"this corruptible shall have put on incorruption, and this mortal shall have put on immortality, then shall be brought to pass the saying that is written, Death is swallowed up in victory"* (I Cor. 15:54).

Since the fall in the garden of Eden, man has constantly attempted to reestablish paradise but without the Tree of Life, i.e., Jesus Christ. Man has ever failed, as fail he must!

Now, even more regrettably, a great segment of the modern church is promoting the "social justice message." This, in effect, teaches that the church will Christianize society in all the nations of the world and, consequently, usher in the kingdom. Such sounds good only to the carnal ear.

In truth, this teaching is not found in the Bible and is, in fact, the opposite of the teaching of Scripture. To be sure, such is going to be brought about but not by a gradual process, with society being gradually Christianized, but instead, it will be cataclysmically changed with the second coming of Christ (Rev., Chpt. 19).

The Scripture teaches, in essence, that while the power of the change, namely in Christ, will be brought about immediately, the effects of the change will be gradual (Dan. 2:44; Isa. 9:7).

Through the dream that God gave to Nebuchadnezzar, with Daniel interpreting it, we know that this world's evil society is going to be smitten by *"the stone,"* which comes from heaven, who is Christ (Dan. 2:34, 45).

Let it ever be understood, God cannot use anything that is devised by man. He can only use that which is birthed by the Holy Spirit, brought forth by the Holy Spirit, and carried out by the Holy Spirit.

While the Lord uses men, the origination of all direction must be strictly from God.

YOUR WILL BE DONE IN EARTH, AS IT IS IN HEAVEN

It should be obvious that the will of God is not being done on earth presently as it is in heaven.

It is not the will of God for all the sin that causes all heartache, pain, and suffering. As well, it is not His will for sickness to ravage the human frame. Neither is death His will, as we have already stated. This would also hold true for poverty, for war, etc.

In truth, almost nothing that is done in the world, or the church for that matter, is His will. While it is true that some few people attempt to carry out His will with all their strength, still, that number is small, and has always been small.

There are several things about the will of God that are supposed to become a part of the Christian experience.

THE WILL OF GOD

Every believer should want, desire, and ardently seek the will of God in all things; however, if the Word of the Lord has already promised us something, then it's not proper for us to ask for those things and then close our prayer by saying, "If it be Your will." He already has told us in His Word exactly what His will is. For us to add "if" to our prayer in this regard means we actually are questioning the Word of God, which no believer desires to do.

For instance, we are not to ask the Lord to save souls if it be His will! We know what His will is regarding salvation. As well, when it comes to divine healing, I believe it is always God's will to heal the sick. I cannot see how that God can get glory out of sickness, but I definitely can see how He gets glory out of healing. However, while it definitely is His will to heal, at the same time, there are times it is not His wisdom to do so. It's like a person desiring to help someone, but things they are doing closes the door. Sometimes there is nothing negative that we know, but God in His own wisdom, and for our good I might quickly add, doesn't do some things we would like for Him to do.

Christ prayed for the will of God to be done in totality and by all individuals on earth. One day very soon that prayer will be answered. It will be during the coming kingdom age. We should pray accordingly.

GIVE US THIS DAY OUR DAILY BREAD

This is a petition for both natural bread and spiritual bread, who is Christ. Notice it says *"daily,"* which applies to both types of bread.

Having accepted Christ as their Saviour, many Christians leave Him there, foregoing that which He desires to be to us each and every day. An example is the manna that was given in the Old Testament and was a type of Christ (Ex., Chpt. 16).

In the giving of the manna, it was on a daily basis, with the exception of the Sabbath. Regarding that, twice as much was given on Friday in order to sustain the Sabbath.

The Lord could have given the manna any way He desired, but He chose to do it in this manner because it was a type of Christ, who is needed on a daily basis in our lives.

As well, if much manna was gathered, with the idea in mind that one would not have to gather it the next day, it would breed worms and stink. Consequently, the importance of the *"daily"* sustenance was magnified each day (Ex. 16:13-36).

Many Christians are attempting to live on manna received yesterday or even many days before. Then they wonder why there are problems in their lives. Jesus on a daily basis will lessen such, or else, give strength to overcome.

In this petition, the natural bread is held up as a necessity, as is obvious, and portrays God as the divine benefactor who provides such for His believing children.

Consequently, whatever is needed should be asked for on a daily basis.

AND FORGIVE US OUR TRESPASSES AS WE
FORGIVE THOSE WHO TRESPASS AGAINST US

This statement by Christ, *"Forgive us our trespasses* (debts),*"* denigrates the false teaching of sinless perfection, despite our great struggles to attain this worthy goal. To be sure, that day will come when *"corruption will put on incorruption,"* but until then, the struggle between the flesh and the spirit continues.

Actually, despite his best efforts, the Christian is continually coming short of the glory of God (Rom. 3:23). Consequently, as we daily ask Him for bread, we are, as well, to ask Him for forgiveness.

However, as is plainly obvious, His forgiving us is tied to our forgiving others their trespasses against us, whether they ask or not. To be sure, the only type of forgiveness that Christ will recognize is the same type of forgiveness that He gives us.

THREE DIFFERENT GREEK
WORDS FOR FORGIVENESS

The first Greek word is *charizomai* and means "to be gracious" or "to give freely." It is used in the sense of "forgive" (II Cor. 2:7, 10; 12:13; Eph. 4:32; Col. 2:13; 3:13).

The word is also used in regard to canceling a debt, as Christ here used it, a concept analogous to forgiving a sin (Lk. 7:42-43).

Paul not only urged the church at Corinth to be gracious to a repentant one who had sinned seriously (II Cor. 2:7-10), but he also insisted that the believers in every church show the same compassion to each other that God had shown in forgiving them: Bear with each other and forgive whatever grievances you may have against one another. Forgive as the Lord forgave you (Eph. 4:32; Col. 2:13; 3:13).

Another Greek word is *aphiemi* and is used in the sense of forgiveness of sins, debts, and crimes. However, the meaning is extended to convey more than mere forgiveness, but also means to dismiss, release, leave, or abandon the claim altogether.

DIVINE FORGIVENESS

Divine forgiveness does not overlook sin or dismiss it lightly, but rather forgiveness is an act of God by which He deals not only with our guilt but with sins themselves. In forgiveness, God removes the sins and makes the guilt moot. No wonder the teachers of the law objected when Jesus said to a paralytic, *"Your sins are forgiven"* (Mk. 2:5). The offended onlookers thought angrily, *"Who can forgive sins but God alone?"* However, He could do so because He is God. (Mk. 2:7)

You and I may be compassionate to another who falls, but we cannot remit his sins. However, God not only forgives sins but, as well, remits or cancels them as if they never happened.

FREEDOM AND RELEASE

Aphesis is another Greek word that speaks of remission of sins (Mat. 26:28; Mk. 1:4; 3:29; Lk. 1:77; 3:3; 24:47; Acts 2:38; 5:31; 10:43; 13:38; 26:18; Eph. 1:7; Col. 1:14; Heb. 9:22; 10:18).

It also is rendered freedom and release (Lk. 4:18).

The preaching of the early church always linked forgiveness with Jesus. He alone is able to give repentance and forgiveness of sins to Israel and all others (Acts 5:31).

The death and resurrection of Jesus put the promises of the Old Testament prophets in perspective, for all the prophets testify about Him that everyone who believes in Him receives forgiveness of sins through His name (Acts 10:43).

Paul specifically linked forgiveness with the death of Christ. He announced it twice in rather similar terms:

"We have redemption through His blood, the forgiveness of sins, according to the riches of His (God's) grace" (Eph. 1:7; Col. 1:14).

GOD'S FORGIVENESS IN THE NEW TESTAMENT

Both Testaments extend the promise of forgiveness to the human race. In the Old Testament as well as the New, human beings are recognized as sinners in need of pardon. The Old Testament links God's forgiveness with sacrifices of atonement.

The New Testament relates forgiveness to Jesus, specifically through His sacrificial death, to which the sacrifices of the Old Testament pointed.

The basis on which God can forgive sin and remain righteous has been provided by Jesus' sacrifice of Himself as an atonement in that ultimate sacrifice, to which Old Testament offerings merely pointed. Hebrews says that by one sacrifice, He has made perfect forever those who are being made holy (Heb. 10:14).

TRANSFORMATION

However, Jesus not only forgives sins, but also, through His death at Calvary, He provided us with the possibility of a dynamic inner transformation. Jesus has done a perfecting work for us to make us new and holy; it was not simply a remedial work, wiping out past sins. Consequently, when thinking of forgiveness, it is important to realize that it is simply the doorway through which we pass into a new life. Jesus' sacrifice did take away our sins. They are so completely gone that God no longer recalls them against those whom He has saved, for He says, *"Their sins and iniquities* (lawless acts) *will I remember no more"* (Heb. 10:17).

The blood of Christ is the basis on which God can righteously provide the promised forgiveness (Rom. 3:25-26).

Christ's atoning death is also the basis for our continuing relationship with God (I Jn. 2:1-2). Sadly, all of us stumble and fail at times as we journey in our new life toward holiness, but even though we do fail, we have the promise of forgiveness for every sin. All anyone needs to do is confess his or her sins, and then God will forgive, and the Holy Spirit will keep on working to cleanse from all unrighteousness (I Jn. 1:7-9).

FORGIVING ONE ANOTHER

The New Testament, as Matthew 6:12 emphasizes, places great stress on the importance of forgiving others.

In Matthew, Chapter 18, Jesus tells three stories to illustrate forgiveness.

- He portrays human beings as sheep prone to go astray. When this happens, we are to seek the straying ones. We are to bring the straying ones home, bearing them in our arms and rejoicing. The image is of a forgiveness that frees us from bitterness or incrimination and provides a joy that is able to heal every hurt (Mat. 18:10-14).

- Jesus then spoke of the hurts and sins that mar family relationships, whether church or personal.

- *"If your brother sins against you,"* He began, and then He went on to explain that we are to take the initiative when we are hurt, and we should seek reconciliation. Peter recognized the difficulty of this teaching and objected. He asked how often such hurts should be forgiven. Jesus answered, *"Seventy times seven"*—a phrase indicating unlimited forgiveness (Mat. 18:15, 22).

Following this, Jesus told a parable about a servant with a debt equivalent to staggering sums of money (in modern terms and rates). When the servant could not pay and begged for time, the ruler to whom he owed the sum simply forgave the entire obligation. However, the same servant later demanded the minor amount a fellow servant owed him (equivalent to a few dollars). He actually went so far as to throw the fellow servant into prison for nonpayment. Jesus' intention is clear: we who are forgiven an unimaginable debt by God surely must be so moved by gratitude that we treat our fellowman as we have been treated.

FORGIVE AS YOU ARE FORGIVEN

This theme—forgive as you are forgiven—is often stressed in the New Testament, and the theme has two applications:

- First, God's treatment of us provides an example that we are to follow in our relationships with other persons. We are to be kind and compassionate to one another, forgiving one another, just as Christ in God forgave us (Eph. 4:32).

- The second application seems to introduce a conditional aspect to the promise of forgiveness. In Matthew 6:14-15, we read (which we will comment on directly), *"For if you forgive men their trespasses, your heavenly Father will also forgive you: But if you forgive not men their trespasses, neither will your Father forgive your trespasses."*

  In Mark 11:25, the thought is expressed this way: *"And when you stand praying, forgive, if you have ought against any: that your Father also who is in heaven may forgive you your trespasses."*

THE TWO ASPECTS OF FORGIVENESS

Such passages trouble many. Elsewhere in the Scriptures, forgiveness is spoken as something provided freely through our Lord. It is promised to all who come to Him. How can the gospel offer and these warnings of Jesus both be correct?

The best answer seems to lie in the way forgiveness affects our personality. Just as every coin has two sides, never only one, so forgiveness has two aspects that can never be separated. The two sides of forgiveness are accepting and extending.

The person who accepts forgiveness becomes deeply aware of his own weakness and need. Pride is ruled out as we take our place as supplicants before the Lord. This basic attitude releases us from our tendency to become angry with, or judgmental of, others. We begin to see others as creatures, who are, like us, flawed by weakness.

Rather than react with inflamed pride (He can't do this to me!), we are freed to respond as God does, with loving concern and forgiveness.

It isn't that God will not forgive the unforgiving; it is simply that the unforgiving lack the humble attitude that both permits them to accept forgiveness and frees them to extend forgiveness.

THAT WHICH HAPPENS TO THE
BELIEVER UPON FORGIVENESS

One who accepts forgiveness adopts an attitude toward himself that transforms his or her attitude toward others. The person who accepts forgiveness becomes forgiving.

There are other effects of forgiveness as well. Jesus once confronted a critical Pharisee who observed with contempt the tearful devotion a fallen woman had for Jesus. The Pharisee thought, *"If this man were a prophet, He would know who is touching Him and what type of woman she is"* (Lk. 7:39).

Jesus responded to the Pharisee's unexpressed thought. He told a story of two men in debt to a money lender. The one owed $50 and the other $500 (a dollar was equal to a day's wage). If the money lender should cancel the debts, Jesus asked, *"Which of them will love him most?"* In essence, the Pharisee answered, *"I suppose the one who had the bigger debt canceled"* (Lk. 7:43).

Jesus then nodded toward the weeping woman and confirmed the principle. Her sins were many, but when she was forgiven, she knew the wonder of God's gift of love, and she responded with love.

RELEASED FROM A SENSE OF GUILT

As we meditate on God's forgiveness and realize how much we have been forgiven, love for the Lord is nurtured in our hearts.

The book of Hebrews develops yet another aspect of forgiveness. Paul compares the sacrifice of Jesus with the Old Testament sacrifices that prefigured Him.

Had the earlier sacrifices had the power to make the worshiper perfect, they would have been cleansed once and for all and would no longer have felt guilty for their sins (Heb. 10:2).

Jesus' sacrifice does make us perfect, at least at the time of forgiveness. Through Jesus our sins are actually taken away! Thus, the believer who realizes that he is truly forgiven is released from a sense of guilt and from bondage to past mistakes. Because God has forgiven our sins (Heb. 10:17), we can forget our past. Forgiven, we can concentrate all our energies on living a godly life.

(Most of the thoughts on forgiveness were derived from the teaching of Lawrence O. Richards.)

THE TYPE OF FORGIVENESS TENDERED BY THE LORD

When an individual is forgiven of sin by the Lord, actually being cleansed by the precious blood of Christ from all unrighteousness, it carries the following meaning:

- Every sin is forgiven.

- All guilt is taken away.

- The person is declared innocent.

- The person is then looked at as though he or she has never sinned.

- The individual is looked at by God as absolutely perfect because the individual is in Christ.

GAINED BY FAITH

All of these things we have mentioned, which are the most wonderful, the most gracious, the most eternal, the most miraculous, and the most stupendous things that one could ever know, are gained solely by faith. In other words, one places one's faith exclusively in Christ and what Christ has done for us at the Cross.

All of this that we have listed becomes that of the person and does so instantly. It cannot be earned, purchased, merited, or gained any other way, only by simple faith in Christ (Jn. 3:16; Eph. 2:8-9; Rom. 6:1-14; I Cor. 1:17-18, 23; 2:2; Gal., Chpt. 5; 6:14; Col. 2:10-15).

TESTING

"And lead us not into temptation, but deliver us from evil: for Yours is the kingdom, and the power, and the glory, forever. Amen" (Mat. 6:13).

Verse 13 has been misunderstood by many, thinking that God, at times, leads us into temptation. That is not the idea at all!

The word *temptation,* as used here, actually means "testing" and should have been translated accordingly.

Peter boldly challenged testing and fell. The instructed child prays that he may not be tested.

As well, the verb "to lead" is not the same word as Matthew 4:1, but instead, suggests the leading of self-confidence.

The idea is: "In my self-confidence, which stems from the flesh and not the Holy Spirit, please do not allow me to be led into testing, for I will surely fail!"

The phrase, *"But deliver us from evil,"* actually says several things:

SATAN

This is evil from the Evil One himself, Satan, and is designed to destroy. It speaks of a cleverly designed trap put together by all the subtly of Satan and is powerful indeed!

Nevertheless, the prior phrase, *"And lead us not into temptation,"* lets us know that God draws the parameters exactly as He did for Job when Satan desired to do certain things to him (Job, Chpt. 1).

Satan, no doubt, desires many things against believers, especially those who are doing him great damage; however, the Lord never allows him the latitude. Satan designs the temptation for our destruction, while the Lord allows it, at least up to a certain point, as a part of our spiritual growth. So, the prayer is that the Lord would allow only small parameters.

DELIVERANCE

The word *deliver* is used because it signifies a snare or trap set by the Evil One, in which the individual, at least on his own, cannot extricate himself. Consequently, he must be delivered by the power of God.

Regrettably, the modern church, at least for the most part, knows little or nothing about deliverance. Man does not need treatment; he needs deliverance.

If it is to be noticed, Jesus said that the Spirit of the Lord had anointed Him to *"preach deliverance to the captives"* (Lk. 4:18). What did He mean by that?

When I, as a preacher of the gospel (or any believer), point the person to Jesus Christ and the sacrifice that He made at Calvary's Cross, understanding that the Cross of Christ is the means by which all things are given to us (I Cor. 1:17-18, 23; 2:2), I am then showing the person how to be delivered.

When his faith is anchored squarely in Christ and the Cross, then the Holy Spirit, who is God, will begin to help him as never before.

Please understand the following: Satan and his minions of darkness are far more powerful than we are, but he most definitely doesn't hold a candle, so to speak, to the Holy Spirit.

Please understand that the Holy Spirit, who is God, who wants to help us, who wants to give us victory, and who wants to get all sin out of our lives, works entirely within the parameters of the finished work of Christ, which gives Him the legal means and right to do all that He does (Rom. 8:1-11).

That's the way that all are delivered, and that's the only way that all are delivered. There is no other way as there need be no other way.

SPIRITUAL

These areas of testing or temptation fall into many and varied categories. Even though they may and, in fact, do affect the domestic, physical, and financial, still, the source is spiritual. As such, it can only be addressed spiritually. Regrettably, the modern church attempts to address these situations with psychology. Such is not possible!

In these situations, whether realizing it or not, one is dealing with demon spirits or some other types of satanic minions of darkness (Eph. 6:10-18). These powers—and powers they are—do not respond to man's machinations. They respond only to the name of Jesus.

Please understand that the very name *Jesus* means "Saviour," which addresses the Cross. However, in the modern church, Freud has taken the place of Philemon, and Maslow has taken the place of Matthew, with Rogers taking the place of Romans. These names, other than the Bible, are noted psychologists, whether dead or alive.

THE KINGDOM OF GOD

The idea is that the kingdom that Jesus mentioned in his prayer does not belong to the Evil One, but instead, to the Lord. In fact, Satan is a usurper attempting to destroy the kingdom that belongs to God. As a result, he has attempted to take the *"power"* and the *"glory."* However, as the kingdom belongs to God, as well, the power and glory also belong to Him.

The word *forever* means that this will never change, despite Satan's attempts, and, in effect, predicts Satan's ultimate doom.

And then, added to the word *forever,* a double guarantee is given by the added word *Amen,* which means "to express a solemn ratification." In other words, in the mind of God, the defeat and destruction of Satan and, therefore, all evil in the world, is a foregone conclusion. As someone has said, "I have read the last page in the Bible, and we win!"

So, as one theologian of the past said, "Inasmuch as this last phrase has guaranteed the whole of the prayer, it could be translated accordingly: 'Hallowed be the name of our God. His kingdom has come; His will is done. He has forgiven us our sins. He has brought our temptation to an end; He has delivered us from the Evil One. His is the kingdom and the power and the glory forever. Amen.'"

You Christian heralds, go proclaim
Salvation through Emmanuel's name!
To distant climes the tidings bear,
And plant the Rose of Sharon there.

God shield you with a wall of fire,
With flaming zeal your breasts inspire,
Bid raging winds their fury cease,
And hush the tempests into peace.

And when our labors all are o're,
Then we shall meet to part no more;
Meet with the blood-bought throng to fall,
And crown our Jesus Lord of all.

THE SERMON
on the
MOUNT

CHAPTER 5

THE MESSAGE

THE MESSAGE

"FOR IF YOU FORGIVE men their trespasses, your heavenly Father will also forgive you" (Mat. 6:14).

WHAT DOES IT MEAN TO TRULY FORGIVE SOMEONE?

The foundation of forgiveness is that of Ephesians 4:32, *"And be you kind one to another, tenderhearted, forgiving one another, even as God for Christ's sake has forgiven you."*

Its superstructure is that of verses 14 and 15. If the super-structure is not visible, its invisibility declares the absence of the foundation; for those who have truly experienced the forgiveness of their sins for Christ's sake do forgive those who sin against them, or else, they stand in danger of losing their souls.

Inasmuch as the matter of forgiveness is so important, the Lord once again addressed Himself to the part of the Lord's Prayer that spoke of forgiveness. As well, He used the word *trespasses*, which speaks of even the largest sins and not just small matters. The idea is this: As God has forgiven us, we are to forgive others. The doing so shows that we fully understand just how much He has forgiven us, even of serious matters. If one does not understand that, one is not truly saved, or else, he has forgotten the pit from which he was dug (Ps. 40:2). If he does understand it, he will be quick to forgive others. Regrettably, these two verses of Scripture (vv. 14 and 15) portray to us that many, if not most, who call themselves Christians are not truly believers.

What does it mean to truly forgive someone? It means to forgive them exactly as God forgave and forgives us.

Let me say it again: For a person to understand forgiveness, I think he has to have at least a modicum of understanding as it regards the Cross of Christ. As we look at faith, for faith to be faith—at least that which God will recognize—it must always be faith in the Cross of Christ, which is faith in the Word. In fact, the entirety of the Bible from Genesis 1:1 through Revelation 22:21 is the story of Jesus Christ and Him crucified.

When faith is mentioned, it always has to have as its object the Cross of Christ, for it is there that every victory is won.

PROBATION

For instance, what type of forgiveness would it be if the Lord said, "I forgive you, but every so often, I will bring up the wrongdoing you committed and hold it over your head so that you will never forget it, and you will, therefore, be constantly reminded of how undependable you really are!"

In truth, such forgiveness would be no forgiveness at all. And yet, that is the type of forgiveness in which most Christians engage themselves.

As another example, what type of forgiveness would it be if the Lord said, "I forgive you; however, I am going to put you on probation for a particular period of time, and if you come through that probationary period satisfactorily, I will review your situation again and determine if restoration is then possible!"

Again, what kind of forgiveness would that be?

Actually, it is no forgiveness at all, and yet, it is the type of forgiveness in which most religious denominations engage, and, therefore, their followers do the same. Such breeds hypocrisy and self-righteousness, which portrays a total departure from the Word of God. It is a travesty of scriptural grace that excludes the very foundation of true Bible Christianity, which is love, mercy, and compassion. Forgiveness by and through Jesus Christ means forgiveness arising from all that He is and all that He does.

Forgiveness rests totally on the atoning work of Christ, that is to say, it is an act of sheer grace all made possible by the Cross. Therefore, forgiveness is rooted in the nature of God as gracious, and upon the fact of true repentance, it is always instantly given.

QUESTIONS

"But if you forgive not men their trespasses, neither will your Father forgive your trespasses" (Mat. 6:15).

Once again, let's look at the Cross: The Cross made possible every single thing that we receive from the Lord. Absolutely nothing has ever come to the sinner or the believer except it came through the great sacrifice of Christ.

The entirety of the Bible in every capacity points toward the Cross of Christ. In fact, the Cross is the centrality of the gospel.

Perhaps a series of questions with answers provided will hopefully shed more light on this all-important subject.

Q: Are Christians to forgive people who have wronged them when they do not ask for forgiveness or even consider they have done wrong?

A: Yes! The forgiveness process is not only for the offender but, as well, for the offended. The offended is to forgive in order that ill feelings or a vengeful spirit not arise within his heart. In other words, forgiveness is just as much for the one who has been wronged as the one who has done the wrong.

As well, upon doing this, we are fulfilling Christ's command to *"Love your enemies, bless them who curse you, do good to them who hate you, and pray for them who despitefully use you, and persecute you"* (Mat. 5:44).

Q: What happens if a believer refuses to forgive?

A: All fellowship and communion with the Lord comes to an abrupt halt. Upon our refusal to forgive, the Lord immediately refuses His forgiveness for us as well! As is obvious, this means that all sins we commit remain against us, with no prayers being answered. It is a chilling prospect! Sadly, this involves far more Christians than one realizes.

Q: If a believer continues in this posture of unforgiveness, will he ultimately lose his soul?

A: The Lord alone has to be the judge; however, Matthew 18:15-17 tells us that such a person becomes a heathen to us. If that is the case with the former believer, it is the case with God as well! However, this does not mean that we should discontinue loving the person and praying for him. In fact, we must forgive even though fellowship is discontinued.

Q: How far should forgiveness be extended, such as the case of something as serious as child molestation, etc.?

A: While forgiveness of such a one certainly must be carried out, still, correct precautions must be carried out simply because an innocent victim or victims is at stake.

In other words, if one were guilty of such a crime and then asked for forgiveness, it must be given; however, such a person must not be placed in charge of children.

If that person is truly sincere and truly wants forgiveness and has been forgiven, he will not even desire to be placed in such a position.

Knowing the consequences of such actions, one surely would not desire his child, or himself for that matter, to be placed in a situation where further acts of abuse could be carried out. This means the law of the land must be carried out as well.

Also, as stated, the offender (that is, if truly repentant) will understand such matters and will not at all blame the persons involved for such actions.

Q: If someone truly repents and, thereby, asks for forgiveness, how should one conduct oneself toward that person?

A: Our attitude toward that person should be—and, in fact, must be—exactly as God's attitude toward him and us. We should conduct ourselves toward him as if nothing ever happened in an adverse manner, with the exception of some situations as addressed in the previous question. Even then, they should be treated with kindness and love, although with proper precautions taken.

Q: Would not a probationary period of time be proper?

A: If that were the case, everybody in the world would be on probation. No! There is nothing in Scripture that even remotely suggests such a thing. As we have previously stated, what if the Lord did us that way when we go to Him and ask for forgiveness? Once again, the type of forgiveness we are to offer to others—and without fail—is the type of forgiveness that God offers to us. No other type will be entertained or accepted by the Lord.

Again, if the sin involves those who are helpless, such as children who consequently cannot help themselves, they must be protected, as stated, at all cost. Nothing must be done that would subject a child to abuse of any nature. So, when decisions are made in these capacities, the safety and the protection of the helpless and the innocent must be given primary consideration.

Q: What does it mean to forgive as God forgives?

A: The only type of forgiveness God will honor is the type that looks upon the offender, who has properly repented, as if his sin was never committed. That is the way the Lord looks at us, and that is the way He demands that we look at others who truly repent.

While it may not be possible for us to truly forget as the Lord truly forgets, still, if we properly understand how much the Lord has forgiven us, or at least have a modicum of understanding regarding such, it will then become much easier to put out of our minds what the other individual has done to us.

When one considers that Christ again broached this subject of forgiveness, even after mentioning it in His prayer, then we begin to understand just how serious this matter really is. Every believer should readily take it to heart!

I personally feel that a believer cannot readily understand biblical forgiveness unless such a believer understands the Cross of Christ as it regards not only our salvation, but above all, our sanctification. In fact, if proper understanding respecting the Cross of Christ relative to sanctification is not held by the believer, an understanding of the Word of God in its entirety will be somewhat lacking. No, I am not suggesting that one cannot understand anything of the Word without the proper understanding of the Cross, but I am stating that this under-standing is absolutely necessary if we are to readily grasp the fundamentals of the Word.

FASTING

"Moreover when you fast, be not, as the hypocrites, of a sad countenance: for they disfigure their faces, that they may appear

unto men to fast. Verily I say unto you, They have their reward" (Mat. 6:16).

In verses 16 through 18, the Lord lays down some rudimentary instructions regarding fasting. Once again, it goes to the heart of the matter instead of the externals.

The phrase, *"Moreover when you fast,"* sets no specific time. In other words, one should fast as one feels led of the Lord to do so.

"Be not, as the hypocrites, of a sad countenance," in effect, addresses the Pharisees who made a big show of their fasting in order to cause the people to think of them as very holy. Christ is saying that it doesn't matter what people think, but what God knows, and He knows everything!

As fasting was done by the Pharisees for show, so much in the religious realm falls into this category. It is done for show, whether it be fasting or giving.

APPEARANCE

"For they disfigure their faces, that they may appear unto men to fast," portrays the actions of hypocrisy. In other words, they were playing a part as an actor, which was a cleverly designed charade. In truth, the Lord didn't even enter the picture, with them carrying forth their religious activities in order to *"appear unto men!"*

How much presently in the realm of Christendom is done in order to impress men? I think one would be shocked to realize that this is probably as acute now as then!

"Verily I say unto you, They have their reward," tells us exactly what the Lord thought of their actions.

It should be quickly stated that all things done in the realm of the spiritual must be for the heavenly Father only, or else, it is of no consequence.

Once again, a failure to understand the Cross of Christ always and without fail leads to self-righteousness.

For instance, grace means that whatever needs to be done has already been done by Christ, and we receive it by simply believing in what He has already done. In fact, if we attempt to add our own efforts to the finished work of Christ, we frustrate the grace of God, which guarantees that we're going to fail (Gal. 2:20-21).

If one is fighting and winning, after awhile, one is going to fight and lose. The only fight we are to engage is *"the good fight of faith."*

A MAN-MADE RELIGION

"But you, when you fast, anoint your head, and wash your face" (Mat. 6:17).

The phrase, *"But you,"* is meant to set apart those who are truly God's children in contrast to those who only profess to be but actually aren't. In effect, the Lord was saying that the Pharisees and all who follow in their train are not His children. Their so-called spirituality was man-made religion, which would not and, in fact, could not be accepted by God.

"When you fast," once again, places the frequency in the heart of the individual and not according to some type of rules and regulations.

Actually, there was only one day of fasting each year that was commanded in the law of Moses, and that was on the great Day of Atonement. This was when the high priest went into the Holy of Holies and applied blood to the mercy seat of the ark of the covenant to make atonement for the entire nation of Israel. He only did it on this day. It was then followed by a great feast. However, by the time of Christ, the Pharisees had ruled that two fast days a week should be carried out. In fact, if they were not carried out, the individuals were looked at as spiritually inferior. However, these two fast days a week were strictly man-devised and not God.

LITTLE GODS

Men love to play God! Modern-day Christianity is rife with these little gods.

"*Anoint your head, and wash your face,*" is meant to show the very opposite of that shown by the Pharisees. These two things, the *anointing of the head* and *washing of the face,* were actually symbols of joy. The anointing of the head was to be with oil and was, in effect, a symbol of the Holy Spirit. It meant (at least in this instance) to consecrate a person to God's service. It is taken from Psalms 23:5, "*You anoint my head with oil; My cup runs over.*"

If it is to be noticed, the Lord didn't tell them not to fast these two particular days each week, or any such time frame, but that whenever they did fast, whatever time it was, they were not to appear unto men to fast, etc.

DESIGNED BY THE HOLY SPIRIT

"That you appear not unto men to fast, but unto your Father who is in secret: and your Father, who sees in secret, shall reward you openly" (Mat. 6:18).

With verse 18, the Lord takes the spiritual activity of fasting completely out of the hands of the Pharisees—where it had been made of none effect—and placed it in its proper position as originally designed by the Holy Spirit.

The Pharisees wanted to appear unto men to fast, while the Lord proclaims the very opposite. It is to be done only to *"your Father"* and is to be done *"in secret."* This was done in order to assuage spiritual pride, which had so occupied the Pharisees. Tragically, it occupies many today as well.

"And your Father," is meant to imply that God was not the *"Father"* of the Pharisees and will not be the *"Father"* of any who follow in their train. Therefore, one can follow man or follow God but cannot follow both!

"Who sees in secret, shall reward you openly," refers to the Father and what He will do for those who truly follow Him instead of following man.

THE FOLLOWING OF MAN OR THE LORD

Although the text may appear to address itself only to fasting, it rather extends itself to one of, if not the single most important things, in living for God—the following of man or the following of the Lord! Sadly, most of Christendom follows men. If they continue to do so, they will see their spirituality gradually, or even speedily, degenerating into religion.

While godly men are certainly to be respected and, in a sense, followed, the individual must be versed enough in the Bible so that he will always know what is right and wrong and will follow accordingly.

Tragically, as with the Pharisees of old, many, if not most, Christians follow their religious denomination, irrespective of its scriptural direction. Such has led millions to hell, and such is leading millions astray at present.

IS FASTING A MEANS OF VICTORY OVER SIN?

Many, possibly even millions of Christians, have been led to believe that one can fast one's way to spiritual victory. In other words, the way to have victory over sin and over the powers of darkness is to fast so many days.

While fasting most definitely is scriptural and most definitely will be a blessing to the individual, that is, if it's led by the Lord, there is no place in the Bible that tells us that fasting will break the powers of darkness and give us victory over sin. Victory over the world, the flesh, and the Devil can come about only by and through the Cross of Christ. In other words, it is the Cross alone that deals with sin (Heb. 10:12; Rom. 6:1-14; 8:1-11; I Cor. 1:17-18, 23; 2:2; Col. 2:10-15).

The church is constantly endeavoring to come up with one fad after the other in order to address the terrible problem of sin, and most definitely sin is the problem. However, there is only one answer for the sin question, and I mean only one, as stated, and that is the Cross of Christ.

CHRIST, THE CROSS, AND THE HOLY SPIRIT

The following might help the believer to understand it a little better:

- Jesus Christ is the source of all things we receive from God (Jn. 1:1-2, 14, 29; 3:16; Col. 2:10-15).

- Though Jesus Christ is the source, the Cross of Christ is the means, and the only means, by which all of these things are given to us (I Cor. 1:17-18, 23; 2:2; Gal., Chpt. 5).

- With Christ being the source and the Cross the means, the Cross of Christ must be the object of our faith, and the only object of our faith (Rom. 1:14; Gal. 6:14; Col. 2:10-15).

- With Christ as the source, the Cross as the means, and the Cross as the object of our faith (and the sole object of our faith), then the Holy Spirit, who works exclusively within the parameters, so to speak, of the finished work of Christ, will work mightily on our behalf. Otherwise, we seriously hinder His work within our lives (Rom. 8:1-11; Eph. 2:13-18).

TREASURES

"Lay not up for yourselves treasures upon earth, where moth and rust does corrupt, and where thieves break through and steal" (Mat. 6:19).

If the eye is set upon treasures in heaven, this single purpose will make the character and life simple and straight, and the Christian will shine for Jesus.

If the eye is set upon treasures on earth, the life and character of the believer will be shrouded in moral darkness. A man's aim determines his character.

If that aim is not simple and heavenward but is earthward and double, all the faculties and principles of his nature will become a mass of darkness. It is impossible to give a divided allegiance.

"Lay not up for yourselves treasures upon earth," concerns itself with far more than the giving of money to the work of God. It concerns itself with the entirety of the lifestyle, aims, and purposes of the believer. Tragically, as the previous admonishing concerning fasting, this one is little heeded either!

Let me say the following about the Cross: In the last 50 or more years, the church has had so little teaching on the Cross of Christ that it little knows its true foundation.

The Message of the Cross of Christ, which, in effect, is the gospel (I Cor. 1:17), is the simplest message there is. Man is lost, and Jesus Christ is the solution. To properly understand the Message of the Cross, we have to think spiritually when our nature is to think carnally.

PROPER OBEDIENCE

Upon proper obedience, the Lord will bless His children respecting financial rewards and the things money can buy, and all other ways as well. Accordingly, it is not wrong for the believer to comfortably provide for his family, etc. However, after this is done, if the Lord has given the individual the ability to make large sums of money, his purpose should be for the spread of the gospel around the world. As a good steward, he should minutely investigate where his money should go and, thereby, diligently seek the mind of the Lord in these all-important matters.

Even though his earthly business may be—fill in the blank—still, his heavenly business should be and, in fact, must be priority.

Sadly, in the far greater majority of the cases, this is little done. Even with money given, most of the time, it is given to worthless projects.

"Where moth and rust does corrupt, and where thieves break through and steal," concerns itself with the *"treasures on earth."*

There is so much good that could be done for the cause of Christ with money placed in the proper hands, but most of the time, moths eat it, and rust corrupts it, with thieves—and we speak of religious thieves—stealing the rest.

TREASURES IN HEAVEN

"But lay up for yourselves treasures in heaven, where neither moth nor rust does corrupt, and where thieves do not break through nor steal" (Mat. 6:20).

"But lay up for yourselves treasures in heaven," is the direct opposite of laying up treasures on earth.

What kind of treasures is the Lord speaking of?

He is speaking of anything that is truly done and carried out for the work of God. Nothing small shall go unnoticed, and nothing large fails to accomplish its purpose, that is, if it is given in the right spirit.

When men ask for an accounting, they are almost all of the time speaking of earthly treasures. However, in this passage, Jesus is asking for an accounting respecting heavenly treasures. It is easy to check up on earthly treasures by looking at a financial statement. It is not so easy respecting heavenly treasures.

There are many who cannot lay up earthly treasures, and, in fact, none should! However, all, irrespective of their state or station in this present life, can lay up great amounts of heavenly treasures.

OUR PRAYER LIFE

All, irrespective of whom they may be, can have an effective prayer life, which is probably the most powerful treasure of all. As well, all can be daily witnesses.

The giving of money to the work of God falls under the category of "all" simply because God doesn't judge us so much on how much we give, but instead, how much we have left (Mk. 12:42).

As someone has said: "It's not what you would do with the million should riches ere be your lot, but what you are doing at present with the dollar and a quarter you've got."

And yet, small amounts, though greatly honored by God, cannot usually perform great works for the Lord due to the smallness. Therefore, for those whom the Lord has blessed with great business ability, they must, in turn, bless the work of God by using it accordingly.

As well, when those who have large sums give only a small amount, let not those persons think that they will be blessed. They won't!

THE HEART

"For where your treasure is, there will your heart be also" (Mat. 6:21).

In the verse just quoted, the Lord is speaking to each person individually. He speaks of *"your treasure"* and asks where it is. Wherever it is, earth or heaven, there the heart will be also.

This does not necessarily mean that one should sell everything he has and give it to the work of God, but instead, he should use the increase for God's work.

Too many times, Christian businessmen continue to invest heavily in earthly risks while giving the Lord a pittance until eventually, thieves, in one way or the other, cause it all to be lost.

If the heart is where it truly ought to be, one will seek the Lord earnestly about any and all transactions, directions, and investments. If that is done with a heart desiring to carry out the will of God, the Lord will lead and guide, with great benefit, not only for the believer, but for the work of God as well! It has been well said, "You cannot outgive God."

THE EYES

"The light of the body is the eye: if therefore your eye be single, your whole body shall be full of light" (Mat. 6:22).

"The light of the body is the eye," is used metaphorically, which is a figure of speech in which a word or phrase is used in place of another to suggest a likeness or analogy between them. Jesus was, in effect, saying that the light of the soul is the spirit.

The phrase, *"If therefore your eye be single,"* means that the spirit of man should have but one purpose, and that is to glorify God. The soul is the part of man that feels (Job 14:22), while the spirit is the part of man that knows (I Cor. 2:11).

"Your whole body shall be full of light," in effect, says that if the spirit of man is single in its devotion to God (meaning not divided), then all of the soul will be full of light.

THE EVIL EYE

"But if your eye be evil, your whole body shall be full of darkness. If therefore the light that is in you be darkness, how great is that darkness!" (Mat. 6:23).

The phrase, *"But if your eye be evil, your whole body shall be full of darkness,"* in effect, says, "If the spirit be evil, the entirety of the soul shall be full of darkness."

"If therefore the light that is in you be darkness, how great is that darkness," is a startling statement!

It means that even when right or righteous things come into such a person's spirit, because of the darkness of his spirit, such righteousness is turned to unrighteousness. Because his *"eye"* is evil, his spirit is evil, and everything about him is evil, even that which should be right.

In other words, when he hears the Word of God in any form, which is light, because of his evil spirit, it is twisted and perverted to mean something that, in fact, it does not mean.

This is the reason that appealing only to the intellect by the preacher of the gospel is a fruitless exercise. If the individual is unsaved, everything that goes to his intellect, which is a product of his spirit, is perverted, consequently, perverting the message. Therefore, the spirit of such a person must be seized by the power of the Holy Spirit. This is done through the heart, which is the seat of one's emotions and, in effect, goes to the person's spirit through the soul.

This is the reason that a spiritual experience most, if not all, of the time involves the emotions. Probably one could say that it involves the emotions all of the time, even though it is not evident all of the time (Jer. 4:14).

THE CROSS

If the believer ignores the Cross of Christ and, thereby, attempts to live for God by other means, he could most definitely ultimately lose his way. He will at least be seriously weakened spiritually. It is the Cross of Christ alone that makes it possible for all the great things of God to be given to us. So, if the believer will simply place his or her faith exclusively in Christ and the Cross, and maintain it exclusively in Christ and the Cross, the

Holy Spirit, who is God and who can do anything, will work mightily on his behalf and give him all of the things that God intends for him to have.

The Holy Spirit works exclusively by and through the Cross. In other words, it's the Cross of Christ that makes it legally possible for the Holy Spirit to do all that He does. That's the reason that it is said: *"For the law of the Spirit of life in Christ Jesus has made me free from the law of sin and death"* (Rom. 8:2).

If the believer tries to live for God by any means other than faith in Christ and the Cross, such a believer will be ruled by the sin nature, which will seriously curtail his experience with the Lord and could cause him to lose his way altogether. In fact, millions have lost their way because of this very thing.

EMOTIONALISM?

So, when some modernist preachers claim that it is only emotionalism when a person is moved upon by the Holy Spirit, with them reacting by weeping, etc., those preachers simply do not know what they are talking about. They are portraying a lack of understanding of how the Holy Spirit moves upon the individual. As stated, He does not deal with the intellect, even though the intellect is, in fact, greatly affected, but with the heart (Heb. 10:16). Now, this doesn't mean that every time the Spirit of God deals with a person, he will weep or react emotionally. Some don't, but that is because of their personalities. To be frank, their reaction doesn't have a whole lot to do with the Holy Spirit.

As the Spirit of God deals with an individual, the darkened spirit of man can be liberated and set free. That is the reason that people can be saved without fully understanding, at least at the outset, what has happened to them.

Their spirit, which is the seat of their will and intellect, has been moved upon greatly by the Holy Spirit through the soul, with the emotions of the person affected. This allows the Holy Spirit to instantly drive away the darkness of the spirit. It is called "born again" and instantly replaces the darkness with light.

Ideally, the believer must continue in this mode, with the spirit (eye) single, i.e., undivided toward God in its devotion. However, too oftentimes the spirit of the individual, i.e. eye, does not remain single but, in fact, is allowed to become double in its devotion, which occasions the next verse.

MAMMON

"No man can serve two masters: for either he will hate the one, and love the other; or else he will hold to the one, and despise the other. You cannot serve God and mammon" (Mat. 6:24).

The phrase, *"No man can serve two masters,"* has to do with the singleness of the spirit of man, which has now become double, so to speak. In other words, he is attempting to serve God and the world at the same time. Actually, this is a conflict that rages constantly! Men attempt to hold onto God with one hand, so to speak, while holding onto the world with the other. To be sure, one or the other will have to go.

"For either he will hate the one, and love the other; or else he will hold to the one, and despise the other," portrays the ultimate conclusion of that individual.

Regrettably, many, if not most, let go of God instead of the world while continuing to serve the Lord in name only!

"You cannot serve God and mammon," is flat out stated as an impossibility.

So, it is total devotion to God or ultimately, it will be total devotion to the world. This is what Jesus was speaking of when He said, *"So then because you are lukewarm, and neither cold nor hot, I will spew you out of My mouth"* (Rev. 3:16).

The word *mammon*, as here used, refers to an egocentric covetousness that claims man's heart and, thereby, estranges him from God. When a man owns anything, in reality, it owns him.

The word *mammon* is derived from the Babylonian "mimma," which means, "anything at all."

Consequently, it is not speaking only of money, but anything that would come between a person and God.

TAKE NO THOUGHT FOR YOUR LIFE

"Therefore I say unto you, Take no thought for your life, what you shall eat, or what you shall drink; nor yet for your body, what you shall put on. Is not the life more than meat, and the body than raiment?" (Mat. 6:25).

The phrase, *"Therefore I say unto you,"* is meant to refer back to the previous statements concerning the laying up of treasures on earth.

"Take no thought for your life," is strong indeed! It is meant to refer to what we eat, drink, and wear. With the words *"put on"* (referring to the body) applying, as well, to the home we live in, methods of transportation, education, etc., the entirety of the physical and material life is addressed.

No, this does not mean that individuals are not to seek gainful employment or to seek growth for their businesses and, thereby, expect the Lord to do for them what they should be doing for themselves. That is not the thought at all! The idea is that one not spend one's time consumed by worry and care respecting these things, which shows a lack of trust and faith in God.

As an aside, it is ironic that those who truly adhere to the "message of covetousness," as I refer to it, think of little else, while Christ says to *"take no thought."*

PRIORITY

An overemphasis on any subject, which means to place the emphasis contrary to the teaching of the Word of God, constitutes heresy. To explain it in the physical sense, it would refer to an ear on someone's head that is six or seven times larger than the other ear. While it is an ear, still, it is no longer in proportion and, consequently, constitutes a deformity.

"Is not the life more than meat, and the body than raiment?" places the priority where it rightly belongs.

Jesus is saying that one's life is far more than mere things, such as fine food and beautiful clothes. Those things are, in fact, necessary, but only in their proper proportion.

The Lord is attempting to lead men away from these things, which are, in fact, necessary, but definitely not the most important. And yet, almost all the world centers up on *things* while neglecting the far more significant purpose of life, which pertains to God and His work.

It is understandable that the world would place the emphasis on things, but not so understandable when that which purports to be the gospel does the same thing. Then the eye (spirit) becomes double, while the body (soul) is filled with darkness!

A PERSONAL EXPERIENCE

Sometime back, while Frances and I were in California, I happened to hear part of a message over television by a noted preacher.

He was explaining the "blessing of Abraham" and very dogmatically stated that it had nothing to do with spiritual things but concerned itself altogether with money. He said the blessing of Abraham was material riches.

I found myself standing in the middle of the floor shouting at the television set and saying, "No! That is untrue."

Whether he knew it or not, he was denying the real purpose for which Christ came, which is the salvation of man from sin. The blessing of Abraham is justification by faith (Gen. 15:6; Gal. 3:14) and has nothing to do with material riches.

While Abraham was most definitely blessed by the Lord in a financial and economic sense, even as every believer should and can be blessed, still, to corrupt the Word of God in the fashion this man did borders on blasphemy.

Once again, the priority is all wrong!

THE CROSS OF CHRIST

Most of the time, and maybe one could say all of the time, when people get off track, it is because they have an erroneous understanding of the Cross of Christ. We must understand as believers that the power of death before the Cross extended even to hell itself. In fact, all of the underground region, even that which was referred to as paradise, was a part of hell. While paradise was altogether different than the burning side of hell, still, it all came under the same auspices (Lk. 16:19-31). Today, due to what Jesus did at the Cross, the paradise side of hell is empty.

When Jesus died on the Cross, He destroyed the power of death held by Satan. He settled the terrible sin debt and, thereby, liberated these righteous souls from paradise (Eph. 4:8-10).

Due to the sin debt being settled at the Cross, when a saint of God now dies, his soul and spirit immediately go to heaven to be with Christ (Phil. 1:23), which means the power of death is now broken.

FAITH

"Behold the fowls of the air: for they sow not, neither do they reap, nor gather into barns; yet your heavenly Father feeds them. Are you not much better than they?" (Mat. 6:26).

In effect, according to this Scripture, the great emphasis of the message of covetousness shows a lack of faith instead of the opposite as constantly claimed!

"Behold the fowls of the air," is meant to draw attention to that which is at least a smaller part of God's great creation.

The phrase, *"For they sow not, neither do they reap, nor gather into barns,"* is meant to portray the absolute lack of that on which man spends much, if not most, of his time.

Once again, the Lord is not demeaning honest industry, especially considering that the very *image of God* calls for such, at least as far as man retains that image! It is the absolute priority on such that is commanded by the Lord to the exclusion of the true mission of man, which is to serve his Creator.

As we deal with faith, before the Cross, people were saved in the same manner we are saved now, which is by faith. Their faith, in essence, was centered in the Cross, typified by the sacrifices, with our faith now centered in the Cross, which has been accomplished.

In essence, one might say that before the Cross, believing sinners were saved by looking forward to a prophetic Jesus, while we are now saved by looking backward to a historic Jesus.

Both ways, however, centered up at the Cross.

OUR HEAVENLY FATHER

The phrase, *"Yet your heavenly Father feeds them,"* proclaims an orderly system set up by the Creator in order that even the lowest forms of His creation would be provided for, which they are.

In effect, the Lord was saying that if the Creator would do such with birds of the air, which are relatively insignificant in the total understanding of things, how much more would He see to the same needs of His highest creation, which is man?

The question, *"Are you not much better than they?"* proclaims man's true worth and sets him apart from the animal kingdom, which completely debunks the foolishness of humanistic evolution.

Such is meant to portray trust that one should have in God, and more than all, it pertains to His children. Actually, He is not speaking of mankind in general, even though some provision has been made for them, as is obvious, but more particularly, to those who call Jesus, "Lord."

TRUST

"Which of you by taking thought can add one cubit unto his stature?" (Mat. 6:27).

Once again, our Lord is teaching trust!

One is to be diligent, industrious, and energetic, respecting all efforts in this realm, and then leave the rest to God. To fret, worry, and live in anxiety shows a lack of faith and constitutes sin (Rom. 14:23).

WORRY AND THE CROSS OF CHRIST

The problems of worry and excess concern have undoubtedly plagued every single believer at one time or another; however, despite the fact that it has and does, worry shows a lack of trust in the Lord, as I think should be obvious. It also shows a lack of love. If we trust the Lord as we ought to and love Him as we should, there will be no worry.

It is impossible for any believer to live a life of trust and obedience, in other words, a life free of worry, care, and concern, unless such a believer understands the Cross as it regards our sanctification, i.e., how we live for the Lord on a daily basis. I don't care how many formulas preachers may give you or how many things they claim will give you the answer. Truthfully, there is only one answer.

That answer is the believer placing his or her faith exclusively in Christ and what Christ has done for us at the Cross and not allowing it to be moved to something else (Rom. 6:1-14; I Cor. 1:17-18, 23; 2:2).

PERSONAL EXPERIENCE

I personally know what it is to try to live this Christian experience and not understand the Cross as it regards our daily life and living.

Yes, a person can be saved without fully understanding the Cross in regard to sanctification. A person can be baptized with the Holy Spirit and fall into this category, and to be sure, a person can even be used of God, and sometimes greatly so, without understanding this of which we say.

However, one cannot live a victorious, overcoming Christian life without understanding the Cross of Christ as it refers to our sanctification. We're speaking of how we live for God on a daily basis, how we grow in grace and the knowledge of the Lord, and how we have victory over the world, the flesh, and the Devil.

I recall those days when I had a lack of understanding, but it is not with gladness. How many nights did I lie awake hour upon hour, plagued with care and concern, and it was all because I did not understand fully what Christ had done for me at the Cross! I understood what He did respecting salvation but had no knowledge whatsoever regarding sanctification.

As a result, I did not understand that every single thing that I needed was met at the Cross, and I mean everything. The Cross provided salvation, which, of course, is the greatest thing of all. As well, the Cross made it possible for believers to be baptized with the Holy Spirit and for Him to abide with us and in us forever. Also, the Cross provided for divine healing, blessings, deliverance, and prosperity of every nature, including answers to prayer, fellowship, and communion with the Lord. In fact, the list is endless. There is no limit to the provision of the Cross, and the quicker we understand that, the quicker will be our daily victory.

Being on this side of the proverbial fence now, so to speak (I speak of the side of the Cross of Christ as it refers to our sanctification and everything else we need from the Lord), there is no worry or fear.

The believer cannot fully trust the Lord and cannot fully love the Lord unless such a believer understands the Cross of Christ as it refers to our life and living. The Cross is God's solution to all problems. In fact, the Cross is His only solution. There is no need for another.

WORRY WILL NEVER PRODUCE
ANYTHING THAT IS POSITIVE

"And why do you take thought for raiment? Consider the lilies of the field, how they grow; they toil not, neither do they spin" (Mat. 6:28).

Once again, the Lord used a metaphor to describe that which He was teaching. He asked this question, *"And why do you take thought for raiment?"* simply meaning that worry and anxiety will never produce any. The idea is to trust God, which He further explains.

"Consider the lilies of the field, how they grow," is meant to point to a system that God has devised to ensure its growth and beauty.

"They toil not, neither do they spin," is meant to state that their beauty has nothing to do with their effort but is given completely by the Creator. The idea of the word *spin* refers to something going round and round in a circle because it doesn't know what to do. It is said, "Insanity is doing the same thing over and over and expecting a different outcome."

The emphasis is strong that the Lord will do the same for His children without anxiety, worry, or fear. The idea of the Cross is that if the Lord loved us enough to die on a Cross for us, surely He will provide for us, as ought to be overly obvious. However, we must emphasize the fact that this only pertains to God's children who are truly born again, and not mankind in general.

SOLOMON

"And yet I say unto you, that even Solomon in all his glory was not arrayed like one of these" (Mat. 6:29).

The phrase *"And yet I say unto you,"* is meant to draw attention to the fact that He is removing His statements from the hypothesis of the Pharisees.

"That even Solomon in all his glory was not arrayed like one of these," uses this king as the epitome of glory, which he was. In other words, Solomon, with all the money and wisdom in the world, could not make himself as beautiful as a lowly lily. It is said that the lilies of Israel had brilliant coloring, especially the purple and white Huleh lily found near Nazareth.

As it regards worry, anxiety, and fear, one should do the following (of course, I speak of believers): As we have already stated, it is absolutely imperative that the believer has his or her faith anchored squarely in Christ and the Cross, and maintained squarely in Christ and the Cross.

With that being done, the following now comes into play: The great Prophet Isaiah said that we should put on *"the garment of praise for the spirit of heaviness"* (Isa. 61:3).

With the believer's faith properly placed in the Cross of Christ, when Satan places oppression on the heart of the believer, that believer should start praising and worshipping the Lord. He should do so constantly without stopping, and he will soon find *"the spirit of heaviness"* lifting. The Holy Spirit through the prophet plainly tells us that this is the case. Put on *"the garment of praise for the spirit of heaviness."* That is your answer.

FAITH

"Wherefore, if God so clothed the grass of the field, which today is, and tomorrow is cast into the oven, shall He not much more clothe you, O you of little faith?" (Mat. 6:30).

Instead of *"if,"* the word *since* should be inserted in the phrase, *"Wherefore,* since *God so clothed the grass of the field."* It is meant to portray God's guarantee.

The phrase, *"Which today is, and tomorrow is cast into the oven,"* portrays how inconsequential this part of His creation is, and yet, how much care He expends on it.

In Israel in those days, the baker's furnace was heated at times with grass for fuel.

The question, *"Shall He not much more clothe you, O you of little faith?"* is meant to proclaim God's much greater care over His children.

We are here told the reason for our lack, which is *"little faith."*

One of the Hebrew words to describe faith or faithfulness is *munah* and means "firmness, steadiness, and fidelity."

The Old Testament often uses this word as an attribute of God to express the total dependability of His character or promises.

Once again, let me give you the key to all victory:

- Jesus Christ and His Cross is the source of all victory.

- The Cross is the means (Col. 2:10-15).

- To reap that benefit, we must ever make the Cross of Christ the object of our faith (I Cor. 1:17-18, 23; 2:2; Col. 2:10-15).

- With that being done, the Holy Spirit will work mightily on our behalf, doing what only He can do (Rom. 8:2).

FAITHFUL TO HIS COMMITMENTS

The first use of the Hebrew word *munah*, which refers to faith, is in describing who the Lord is and what the Lord is. It says: *"He is the rock, His work is perfect: for all His ways are judgment: a God of truth and without iniquity, just and right is He"* (Deut. 32:4).

Many other passages apply this great Old Testament term to God or to His words and works (I Sam. 26:23; Ps. 33:4; 36:5; 40:10; 88:11; 89:1-2, 5, 8, 24, 33, 49; 92:2; 98:3; 100:5; 119:75, 86, 90, 138; 143:1; Isa. 11:5; 25:1; Lam. 3:23; Hos. 2:20).

The Greek word for "faith" or "faithful" is *pistos* and means "trusting and believing." It can also be translated "trustworthy, reliable, faithful."

It means that we can trust God to remain faithful to His commitments. As well, in view of the fact that God entrusts so much to us, we are to use our opportunities to show loyalty to Him, and above all, not doubt Him.

Because God is faithful, He can be trusted fully to completely carry out His commitments to us in Christ (I Cor. 1:9; 10:13; II Cor. 1:18; I Thess. 5:24; II Thess. 3:3; II Tim. 2:13; Heb. 2:17; 10:23; 11:11; I Pet. 4:19; I Jn. 1:9; Rev. 1:5; 3:14; 19:11).

TAKE NO THOUGHT ...

"Therefore take no thought, saying, What shall we eat? or, What shall we drink? or, Wherewithal shall we be clothed?" (Mat. 6:31).

The phrase, *"Therefore take no thought,"* means simply to not worry about it in the least!

This verse is similar to verse 25, but yet, with a difference.

The *"take no thought for your life"* in verse 25 concerns a state of anxiety, where this statement in verse 31 actually means that even one anxious thought is forbidden.

So, He is saying that to have even one single thought regarding what we shall eat, what we shall drink, or how we shall be clothed is a waste of time and is forbidden by the Lord.

In view of the fact that He spends so much time in this one area, it shows us that the problem is acute even among God's children. Once again, allow us to emphasize the fact that the Lord is not meaning that we take a cavalier attitude toward such things, but that we should do our very best in these areas and then trust God for the results.

Some who are indolent have erroneously thought that in view of these passages, they do not have to work, etc. However, as stated, this is not the meaning by the Lord at all, for He also says, *"That if any would not work, neither should he eat"* (II Thess 3:10).

YOUR HEAVENLY FATHER

"(For after all these things do the Gentiles seek:) for your heavenly Father knows that you have need of all these things" (Mat. 6:32).

The word *Gentiles*, in the phrase, *"For after all these things do the Gentiles seek,"* is meant to portray all who do not know God and are strangers to the commonwealth of Israel. In effect, the Lord is saying that such do not have the help, care, and promises of the *"heavenly Father"* as do God's children. Consequently, these Gentiles, i.e. unsaved, have to fend for themselves as best as possible. As a result of not having the help of the Lord and because they are not His children, some few of these have their material needs met, while many, if not most, in the world go lacking, and seriously so. Hence, this is the reason for so much poverty, starvation, and dire circumstances.

"For your heavenly Father knows," is meant to express the contrast between those who do not know the Lord and those who do.

To be sure, the Lord knows all things. However, the word *you* in the last phrase, *"That you have need of all these things,"* sets the believer apart as alone the recipient of God's care, oversight, and provision.

What a promise!

SEEK FIRST THE KINGDOM OF GOD ...

"But seek you first the kingdom of God, and His righteousness; and all these things shall be added unto you" (Mat. 6:33).

The phrase, *"But seek you first the kingdom of God, and His righteousness,"* gives the condition for God's blessings.

Inasmuch as the unconverted are not seeking such, it is left up to the believer to do so and, in turn, receive God's benefits.

As well, we are plainly told here to put the kingdom of God and His righteousness first. This means, as should be obvious, that we are not to spend our time and abilities as the unconverted seeking the things of this world, but instead, we are to attend to God's business first.

How many truly do this?

Of course, the Lord is the only one who truly knows the answer to that question. Nevertheless, I think it is obvious, at least in many, if not most, experiences that the Lord's work comes second or even further down the line, if at all.

Let it be known that all who do such are not only hurting the work of God, but they are short-changing themselves as well.

"And all these things shall be added unto you," is the guarantee of God's provision. And what a provision it is! However, we should understand that *"all these things"* are the things the Lord desires that we have and not many things that some of us foolishly desire.

TAKE NO THOUGHT ...

"Take therefore no thought for the morrow: for the morrow shall take thought for the things of itself. Sufficient unto the day is the evil thereof" (Mat. 6:34).

The phrase, *"Take therefore no thought for the morrow,"* is meant for us to direct our attention to the cares of the present day and not be in anxiety over the future.

"For the morrow shall take thought for the things of itself," is meant to refer back to verse 27.

No matter how much we may be concerned about a situation and may spend sleepless nights over it, all of the fretting, worry, and anxiety will not change anything. However, faith in God can change it. This is the idea of that phrase.

"Sufficient unto the day is the evil thereof," means that we should handle daily difficulties in faith and have faith for the future that the present difficulties will not grow into larger ones.

We have God's assurance that they won't, that is, if we will sufficiently believe Him.

A PERSONAL EXPERIENCE

Demonic oppression and depression is a very serious thing, as should be obvious. I suppose one can say without fear of contradiction that every single human being, even all believers, experience oppression and even depression in some form in their life and living. It is like a hundred pounds is placed on one's shoulders, which weighs down the individual, with everything looking dark. Perhaps that somewhat explains what oppression or depression is.

Sometime back while preaching on a Sunday morning at Family Worship Center, it dawned on me that since the Lord began to open up to me the Message of the Cross back in 1997,

I have not suffered an oppressive spirit from that day until this. That is now a time frame of approximately some 20 years, and I have not had one moment of oppression or depression. Before the revelation of the Cross, it seemed to be a constant process, with the load seemingly getting heavier by the day.

It is said of our Lord: *"How God anointed Jesus of Nazareth with the Holy Spirit and with power: who went about doing good, and healing all who were oppressed of the Devil; for God was with Him"* (Acts 10:38).

As it regards oppression and, of course, depression, as well, man has no cure for this malady. When I say no cure, I mean that man provides no help whatsoever. However, the believer (I said believer) can have total victory in this respect, even as we've already explained. Due to the seriousness of the matter, let me briefly say it again:

- The believer's faith must rest exclusively in Christ and what Christ did for us at the Cross. This is an absolute necessity.

- The believer is then to *"put on the garment of praise for the spirit of heaviness"* (Isa. 61:3). With faith properly placed and praises unto the Lord flowing from one's heart, he will find this *"spirit of heaviness"* lifting and not returning.

When I saw the cleansing fountain,
Open wide for all my sin,
I obeyed the Spirit's wooing,
When He said, Wilt thou be clean?

Though the way seems straight and narrow,
All I claimed was swept away;
My ambitions, plans, and wishes,
At my feet in ashes lay.

Then God's fire upon the altar,
Of my heart was set aflame;
I shall never cease to praise Him,
Glory, glory to His name!

Blessed be the name of Jesus!
I'm so glad He took me in;
He's forgiven my transgressions,
He has cleansed my heart from sin.

Glory, glory to the Father,
Glory, glory to the Son,
Glory, glory to the Spirit,
Glory, to the Three in One.

THE SERMON
on the
MOUNT

CHAPTER 6

CONDUCT

CONDUCT

"JUDGE NOT, THAT YOU be not judged" (Mat. 7:1).

GOD ALONE IS JUDGE

Even though a chapter insertion is placed between the last verse of Chapter 6 and this verse, still, it is all the Sermon on the Mount. Consequently, the statement concerning judging harks back to verses 25 through 34 of the previous chapter.

The idea is that God may permit poverty to test His child, but fellow believers are not to err as Job's friends did and believe the trial to be a judgment for secret sin.

However, the word *judging*, as here used, covers every aspect of dealing with our fellowman.

The entirety of the Bible, both Old and New Testaments, strongly affirms the truth that God alone is qualified to serve as judge. In fact, James basically states this in James 4:12.

GOD ALONE IS QUALIFIED

"*There is one Lawgiver, who is able to save and to destroy* (presents God as the only One who can fill this position)*: who are you who judges another?* (The Greek actually says, 'but you—who are you?' In other words, 'who do you think you are?')" (James 4:12).

All of this tells us that judging is a very serious thing. As well, it screams loud that no human being is qualified to judge another, and by that, I'm speaking of judging the motives of an individual, etc. And yet, even though God is the only competent judge because He alone knows the heart of man, still, the tenor of the Bible proclaims the fact that the Lord is not eager to judge, despite the fact that He is able to judge perfectly. In all of this, we learn from the Word of God that *"the Father judges no man* (judges no one who has come to Christ, for all sin has been settled in Christ)*, but has committed all judgment unto the Son* (Christ is the Saviour today but will be the judge tomorrow)*"* (Jn. 5:22) (The Expositor's Study Bible).

WHY HAS THE FATHER COMMITTED ALL JUDGMENT TO THE SON?

It is because the Lord Jesus Christ paid the price for man's redemption at the Cross of Calvary. This is such a momentous event with such far-reaching effect that it defies all description. And yet, despite having carried out the greatest task known to humanity and, in fact, the greatest that will ever be known, Jesus personally said:

And if any man hear My words, and believe not, I judge him not (means that he is not pronouncing sentence now; He has come as Saviour and, at the present, not as judge): *for I came not to judge the world, but to save the world* (proclaims His present mission, which has lasted now for nearly 2,000 years). *He who rejects Me, and receives not My words, has One who judges him* (presents a truth that the church desperately needs to hear and understand, and the entirety of the world for that matter): *the word that I have spoken, the same shall judge him in the last day* (speaks of the 'judgment seat of Christ' for believers and the 'great white throne judgment' for unbelievers). *For I have not spoken of Myself* (His words are not simply His own, but rather from the Father, i.e., in effect, the entirety of the Godhead); *but the Father who sent Me* (He was sent by the Father for a distinct purpose and mission), *He gave Me a commandment, what I should say, and what I should speak* (in effect, says, 'In rejecting Me and My words, men reject and insult the Father; His Word that they dare to renounce is as solemn and unalterable as the Word spoken on Sinai') (Jn. 12:47-49) (The Expositor's Study Bible).

JESUS CHRIST AS THE JUDGE

And yet, even though Jesus did not come in His first advent to judge mankind, but rather to save mankind, still, there is coming a day that our Lord will serve as the judge of all humanity, both believers and unbelievers. All believers will be judged at the judgment seat of Christ. However, this judgment will not be for sins, that having already been addressed at Calvary, but it will be with regard to motives, intentions, etc. All of that will have to do with the reward or lack of such as it pertains to each and every person.

The great white throne judgment will address all unbelievers. No believers will be present at this judgment (Rev. 20:11-15).

The idea is this: Mankind—and that goes for the entirety of the human race—will face Jesus Christ at Calvary's Cross, where every sin can be forgiven and where eternal life can be granted, or else, they will face Him at the great white throne judgment, but face Him they shall!

MAN-MADE RULES

Paul said, *"Let no man therefore judge you in meat, or in drink, or in respect of an holyday, or of the new moon, or of the Sabbath days"* (Col. 2:16).

These passages do not pertain to such things as alcohol, nicotine, etc., and neither do they pertain to such things as jewelry, etc. But yet, some churches seem to specialize in rules and regulations that they think denote some type of holiness. They don't!

The idea is that particular groups or religious denominations subscribe to certain man-made rules and then judge everyone accordingly. Such denies not only Christian freedom, which Bible Christianity espouses, but above all, the lordship of Christ.

It has always been man's problem, especially religious man, to attempt to usurp authority over the lordship of Christ.

Unless they are especially condemned in the Word of God, all extracurricular activities should be left up to the conscience of each believer.

To be sure, even if made to conform to man-made rules, still, the spiritual condition of such a one is certainly not improved, but instead, oftentimes diminished because of these rules and regulations, whatever they might be. As someone has said, Christ must be Lord of all, or He is not Lord at all.

WHAT ABOUT CHURCH DISCIPLINE THAT CALLS FOR A JUDGMENT?

I Corinthians, Chapter 5, outlines the method of church discipline and the basis on which it is carried out.

This particular case that took place in the Corinthian church involved a man who had taken up with his father's wife (step-mother) (I Cor. 5:1). As well, it seems from II Corinthians 7:12 that the father was alive, for that passage refers to the one *"who suffered wrong,"* as well as the one who had *"done the wrong,"* that is, if the same case is, in fact, being addressed. However, it really makes no difference if it is the same case or not because the principle is the same.

Whenever the news came to Paul concerning this situation, he said, *"For I verily, as absent in body, but present in spirit, have judged already, as though I were present, concerning him who has so done this deed"* (I Cor. 5:3).

It seems from the description (and, no doubt, was) that the individual concerned was refusing to cease such immoral activity or even admit it was wrong. In other words, he was openly practicing immorality, and it seems that some in the church were not too very much concerned about it. Also, there is some indication that he was one of the leaders in the church as well.

Paul judges and says that several things should be done.

CEASE PRAYING FOR THE INDIVIDUAL

In view of this individual refusing to repent and, thereby, cease his immoral activities, the church should *"deliver such an one unto Satan for the destruction of the flesh, that the spirit may be saved in the day of the Lord Jesus"* (I Cor. 5:5). This verse, I Corinthians 5:5, can be addressed in a long lengthy dialogue or by a very short statement, but either way, the meaning will come out basically the same. What Paul was saying is that believers can withdraw all spiritual influence from such an individual— and even cease praying for him—so as to permit Satan to afflict his body or cause other reverses. At times this will cause such a person to be brought to repentance. That's the idea!

FELLOWSHIP WITHDRAWN

The church is not to associate with anyone who calls himself a brother and consistently practices sin. In other words, such a person is not even trying to overcome the problem, whatever it might be, but is openly continuing in a grossly unscriptural manner. Paul says the fellowship should be withdrawn to such an extent that with such a man do not even eat (I Cor. 5:11).

This was to be done by the local church at Corinth, which would be the same for any church because the wrongdoing had taken place there, and the leaders of the local assembly were more qualified, therefore, to judge.

CHURCH DISCIPLINE

There are no perfect people, and there are no perfect churches. So, as it regards church discipline, we must always keep that in mind and do so with it balanced against the Word of God.

In fact, the answer is found in the affirmation of Scripture that God is the ruler of the universe and is the final moral arbiter of all things. He, the judge, had already pronounced His verdict on the practices about which Paul was writing. He had identified these practices as sin, as was given in the Old Testament and carried over, of course, into the New Testament. What the local church is called upon to do is to agree with God in the divine assessment of the actions of this one who calls himself a brother.

If the individual insists upon continuing in the wrongdoing, which means he has no intention of ceasing such activity, the church is to expel or *"put away from among yourselves that wicked person"* (I Cor. 5:13).

Condemning someone by calling into question that person's motives, actions, or personal convictions is vastly different from accepting God's verdict that certain actions are sin, and that those who practice them must be ostracized. There are certain things carried out in I Corinthians, Chapter 5, that give us guidelines as laid down by the Holy Spirit through the apostle.

THE PRACTICE OF SIN

What necessitates discipline is an individual's choice to practice what the Bible identifies as sin. The identifying word in this action is *"practice,"* which is obvious in I Corinthians, Chapter 5. And yet, there is something else that must be said here, which we will address to a greater degree momentarily.

There are millions of believers the world over who do not understand the Cross of Christ as it regards our everyday life and living, which speaks of victory over the world, the flesh, and the Devil. By not understanding this all-important truth that is outlined in Chapter 7 of Romans, such a believer is ruled by the sin nature, despite every effort to overcome certain things, whatever they might be.

He will find himself failing again and again, even with the same sin. That particular individual is not put into the position of purposely practicing sin. There are millions who fall into this category, and I exaggerate not. Discipline is applied only when a person refuses to acknowledge that his practices are sin and refuses to change his ways, or even make any attempt to change his ways.

RESTORATION

However, the goal of all church disciplines should always be church restoration. In the case mentioned by Paul, the situation demanded that such activity cease immediately, or the person must be disfellowshiped. Of course, we continue to speak of the man who was living with his father's wife, actually, his step-mother, with evidence that his father was still alive.

There is evidence that the man repented and ceased his activity. Paul then called on the Corinthians to accept him back and to reaffirm their love for him (II Cor. 2:8).

All of us, in fact, may fail and have to come to the Lord in confession and repentance. For this, there is no call for discipline. Discipline is applied only when a person refuses to acknowledge that his practices are sin and refuses to change his ways.

Yet, in such a case, if the individual refuses to repent even though fellowship will be withdrawn, Paul said, *"Yet count him not as an enemy, but admonish him as a brother"* (II Thess. 3:15).

In other words, everything that is done is done with the thought in mind of the person ultimately repenting and being restored to fellowship.

MORAL FAULT

The occasion for church discipline is found in moral fault—the practice of sin. However, it should be understood that no church discipline is called for respecting the committing of sin, but rather for the practice of sin, as is obvious in these passages. Upon admonishment, if the brother in question had ceased and, thereby, repented before the Lord, no further action would have been called for or needed.

Respecting other deviations, there is little example in Scripture that church discipline is called for. Difference in convictions or even doctrinal differences, unless heretical, do not seem to call for church discipline. It is only the consistent practice of sin without acknowledgment of the fault that occasions discipline.

THE MANNER UNDERTAKEN

The responsibility for such discipline rests on the local Christian body. It is not scriptural for some group, committee, or board many miles away to sit in judgment on these matters. Such deprives the local church of its God-given spiritual authority.

Even though Paul sought the Lord earnestly respecting this situation at Corinth and was given an answer to give to the church, still, it was the local church that carried out these actions as laid down by the Holy Spirit. It was not some group elsewhere. To deviate from these directions is to usurp authority over the Holy Spirit, which God cannot countenance.

As should be obvious, exercising church discipline is very different from adopting the judgmental and condemning attitude against which Scripture speaks.

In scriptural church discipline, we see the loving action of the Christian community, committed to obedience, intending through the discipline to help the brother or sister turn from sin and find renewed fellowship with the Lord.

INSTANT RESTORATION

As well, as is obvious, the moment repentance is engaged by the offending party, which necessitates a ceasing of the sinful practice (whatever it is), the person is to be instantly restored (II Cor. 2:6-7). The idea that some probationary period should be instituted is not found in Scripture and, in fact, is foreign to all scriptural practices, which proclaim the love and grace of God.

Paul told these Corinthians: *"I beseech you that you would confirm your love toward Him"* (II Cor. 2:8). We must always understand that there is no such thing as a probationary justification.

Then Paul said, *"For to this end also did I write, that I might know the proof of you, whether you be obedient in all things"* (II Cor. 2:9).

ON TRIAL

In I Corinthians, the man was on trial, and now the church was on trial! They were to restore this brother immediately, with the understanding that he had truly repented, which means the sinful activity had ceased. If such were not done, one could be *"swallowed up with overmuch sorrow"* (II Cor. 2:7).

Consequently, it should be understood (and is obvious in Scripture) that the Holy Spirit not only takes the discipline seriously, but the restoration as well.

CHRISTIANS RULED BY THE SIN NATURE

This is a problem that most of the modern church understands not at all. As previously stated, there are millions of Christians (yes, millions) who do not understand the Cross of Christ as it regards sanctification. No matter how hard they struggle to overcome sin, such people will be ruled by the sin nature. This means that they will be committing a certain sin, whatever it might be, over and over again. By not understanding the Cross of Christ, which greatly hinders the Holy Spirit, such people are doomed to failure.

In other words, their will power is not enough. As stated, this is not an isolated situation but that which affects untold millions of Christians. With some, it's sins of the flesh, such as alcohol, nicotine, gambling, pornography, drugs, etc. With others, it's sins of the spirit, such as pride, bitterness, unforgiveness, jealousy, etc.

The only answer for this is the Cross of Christ. With the modern church world understanding the Cross of Christ not at all regarding sanctification, this automatically condemns such a person to the rulership of the sin nature.

THE CROSS OF CHRIST
AND VICTORY OVER SIN

That's the reason that Paul said:

Let not sin (the sin nature) *therefore reign* (rule) *in your mortal body* (showing that the sin nature can once again rule in the heart and life of the believer if the believer doesn't constantly look to Christ and the Cross; the 'mortal body' is neutral, which means it can be used for righteousness or unrighteousness), *that you should obey it in the lusts thereof* (ungodly lusts are carried out through the mortal body if faith is not maintained in the Cross [I Cor. 1:17-18]) (Rom. 6:12) (The Expositor's Study Bible).

It's sad to say, but the modern church has adopted humanistic psychology as the answer to the sin question. That's strange considering that psychology doesn't really even believe there is such a thing as sin.

However, irrespective of the labels that psychology may give the problem, the truth is, the problem is sin. Let the reader understand that there is no hope whatsoever from this source. The truth is that man does not need treatment; he needs deliverance. Jesus Christ alone can deliver, and He does so by the power of the Holy Spirit, who works exclusively within the parameters, so to speak, of the finished work of Christ, i.e., the Cross.

It's the Cross of Christ that gives the Holy Spirit the legal means to do all that He does for us and with us (Rom. 8:2). The Holy Spirit actually doesn't demand very much of us, but He does demand one thing, and that is that our faith be exclusively in Christ and the Cross, and maintained exclusively in Christ and the Cross (Rom. 6:1-14; 8:1-11; I Cor. 1:17-18, 23; 2:2; Col. 2:14-15).

TWO DIRECTIONS

I'm going to give you a little diagram that will show you how most of the church world is trying to live for God. Sadly and regrettably, this way brings only defeat:

- Focus: Works

- Object Of Faith: Performance

- Power Source: Self

- Results: Defeat

In the little diagram just given, you are looking at the way that virtually the entirety of the church world is attempting to live for God. Most of it is done out of ignorance, in other words, they simply don't know any other way. So, let's use the same formula, but yet, the way the Scripture teaches us to function God's way:

- Focus: The Lord Jesus Christ (Jn. 1:1-3, 14, 29; 14:6, 20; Col. 2:10-15).

- Object Of Faith: The Cross of Christ (Rom. 6:1-14; I Cor. 1:17-18, 23; Col. 2:10-15).

- Power Source: The Holy Spirit (Rom. 8:1-11; Eph. 2:13-18).

- Results: Victory (Rom. 6:14; 8:2).

MEASURED TO YOU AGAIN

"For with what judgment you judge, you shall be judged: and with what measure you mete, it shall be measured to you again" (Mat. 7:2).

As we have attempted to bring out, other than that which is outlined by the Lord, the believer is never to judge others. The penalties are severe!

"For with what judgment you judge, you shall be judged," proclaims that whatever motive we ascribe to others, such motive will ultimately be ascribed to us.

Likewise, the phrase, *"And with what measure you mete, it shall be measured to you again,"* is meant to impress upon the believer the harshness of what he is doing. The judgment is the verdict; the measure is the severity of the verdict.

To turn it around, the idea is that we are to judge others exactly as we would judge ourselves, for, in fact, that is exactly what we are doing, whether we realize it or not. To carefully weigh the consequences should give us room for pause.

CONSIDER

"And why do you behold the mote that is in your brother's eye, but consider not the beam that is in your own eye?" (Mat. 7:3).

The idea behind these statements points to the Pharisees, who were constantly looking for small infractions of the law, whether real or imagined.

The question, *"And why do you behold the mote that is in your brother's eye?"* is meant to condemn mote hunting. In other words, the believer to whom the Lord is speaking is not to be looking for fault or wrongdoing in the lives of fellow believers.

Inspecting others was a favorite pastime of the Pharisees, and regrettably, it continues presently. The Lord now tells us why we should not do such a thing: This part of the question—*"But consider not the beam in your own eye"*—is meant to proclaim the fact that we have plenty about ourselves that is wrong. This should occupy all of our time in eliminating our wrongs instead of looking for infractions in others. In fact, the mote and beam are contrasted. The constant judging of others portrays the fact that we are much worse off than the one we are judging.

YOUR BROTHER

"Or how will you say to your brother, Let me pull out the mote out of your eye; and, behold, a beam is in your own eye?" (Mat. 7:4).

The question, *"Or how will you say to your brother?"* is meant to impress upon us the seriousness of setting ourselves up as judge, jury, and executioner. Plainly, the impression is that we are not qualified.

"Let me pull out the mote out of your eye," portrays the individual as the Pharisees of old, who constantly knew how to set everyone straight, while he was not walking straight himself.

The conclusion of the question, *"And, behold, a beam is in your own eye?"* once again draws attention to the fact that the person doing the judging is in far worse spiritual condition than the one being judged.

HYPOCRITE

"You hypocrite, first cast out the beam out of your own eye; and then you shall see clearly to cast out the mote out of your brother's eye" (Mat. 7:5).

The phrase, *"You hypocrite,"* aptly describes such a person. He is acting the part without possessing the reality. In other words, what he is claiming that the other person should have done or do, he does not, in fact, possess himself.

The phrase, *"First cast out the beam out of your own eye,"* is meant to proclaim the fact that we constantly have enough faults and even sins within ourselves that should occupy all of our time in elimination.

"And then you shall see clearly to cast out the mote out of your brother's eye," has the emphasis on the word *then.*

When we properly analyze ourselves, then and only then can we see clearly.

If per chance we then see a mote in someone else's eye, we will not at all come from a superior attitude, but will rather deal in kindness and love. Only then can our actions be effective anyway.

The probable intent of Christ in this scenario is that we not censor our brother or sister in any respect, but instead, portray to them a loving example of us handling our own faults in a scriptural way. This will set its own example of righteousness.

In other words, the victories we win in our own lives serve as the greatest examples of all, which eliminates all finger-pointing.

HOLY

"Give not that which is holy unto the dogs, neither cast you your pearls before swine, lest they trample them under their feet, and turn again and rend you" (Mat. 7:6).

Verse 6 tells us that judgment, however, is to be made respecting the actions of the ungodly, and heavenly treasure is not to be exposed to their contempt and hostility. To these, the gospel and the ensuing wrath of God (if they be rejected) are to be preached.

The phrase, *"Give not that which is holy unto the dogs, neither cast you your pearls before swine,"* is speaking of those known to be antagonistic to the gospel and, therefore, its antagonist.

Regrettably and sadly, major religious denominations have at times ignored this command of the Lord and have engaged the news media to carry out the destruction they desired. In these cases, there is little desire with these denominations (whomever they may be) to handle the situation in a scriptural manner, but rather to destroy. As such, the sin becomes abominable.

We must understand that God does not hold man nearly as accountable for his condition—a condition, incidentally, over which he has little control—as he does man's rejection of Christ, who is God's solution to man's dilemma.

THE EVIL OF THE WORLD

The phrase, *"Lest they trample them under their feet, and turn again and rend you,"* proclaims the penalty for such action. It may be awhile in coming, but to be sure, it will come. Then, that which is truly holy, as well as the pearls of the gospel, will be destroyed. That is, if, in fact, any holiness remains.

As stated, it may seem as if the statement of verse 6 has no relationship to the preceding verses concerning judgment, but, in fact, it does. The idea is that even though there are problems in the church, as verses 1 through 5 proclaim, still, the church is never to reach out into the world—the dogs—for help in order to solve its internal disputes.

No, it is not speaking of things akin to Paul's appeal to Caesar because ungodly men in the reprobate Jewish church were attempting to take his life (Acts 25:9-10). In all such actions, the believer—especially if his life is at stake as Paul's was—should take advantage of the laws of the land if, in fact, help can be derived from such.

ASK, SEEK, AND KNOCK

"Ask, and it shall be given you; seek, and you shall find; knock, and it shall be opened unto you" (Mat. 7:7).

The thrust of verse 7 and the following is that in such situations as are common in the church, the believer does not have to go to the world for help, but instead, should seek the Lord for wisdom and guidance in whatever is needed.

The idea is this: Why would the believer go to the world for help in matters pertaining solely to the work of God, especially when the world system has no knowledge of such, when we can easily go to the Lord for whatever wisdom, judgment, or help that is needed?

The phrase, *"Ask, and it shall be given you,"* is also an open invitation for all believers everywhere to *ask* for whatever they need. It implies a heavenly Father who has resources that are inexhaustible.

SEEK AND YOU SHALL FIND

"Seek, and you shall find," is meant to imply that our *asking* may not be immediately answered, with the word *seek* referring to a casting about as to the reason.

Many times, if not all times, the Lord takes advantage of our petitions to straighten out matters within our lives that need attention. As a result, the answer, at least at times, is not immediately forthcoming. That is when the seeking is brought into play, which means to seek the reason the answer is not immediate.

In these occasions, the Lord deals with our hearts, portraying to us areas of spiritual pride, or whatever the problem may be. Therefore, as stated, if the answer does not come immediately, we should seek the Lord as to the reason, which, within itself, is designed to draw us nearer to Him.

KNOCK, AND IT SHALL BE OPENED UNTO YOU

Regrettably, many modern Christians are taught that if the answer is not immediately forthcoming, their faith is deficient. While that may be true at times, the inference is that most of the time, it pertains to something else, such as lack of consecration, wrong direction, or it's not the wisdom of God to grant the request at that time.

At any rate, the believer must not cease his asking but should seek the reason for the delay. It is promised that he will find that reason.

The phrase, *"Knock, and it shall be opened unto you,"* as well, implies a door that does not immediately open. Jesus dealt with this at length in Luke, Chapter 11, which was to a far greater degree than here. We will not now comment on this except to say that if you continue to knock, it shall be opened unto you.

Regrettably, many Christians quit asking immediately before the answer is forthcoming, discontinue seeking just before it is to be found, and stop knocking and, thereby, turn away just before the door opens.

The delay—if, in fact, there is a delay—is for a purpose and is designed by the Holy Spirit for our good and not for our harm.

Going back to the Cross, the Bible doesn't teach sinless perfection (for all the obvious reasons), but it definitely does teach victory over sin in that *"sin shall not have dominion over you"* (Rom. 6:14).

So, that means that no believer should ever be bound by sin in any capacity, should ever be overcome by sin, or should ever practice sin, but he should live a victorious, overcoming, Christian life, which Jesus paid for at the Cross.

The reason for spiritual failure in the heart and life of a believer is because of faith that's improperly placed. In other words, for victory to be ours, our faith must be in Christ and what He did for us at the Cross.

EVERY ONE

"For every one who asks receives; and he who seeks finds; and to him who knocks it shall be opened" (Mat. 7:8).

If one is to notice, the Lord habitually makes certain statements and then turns right around and says the same thing in a different way but with the same meaning and with added emphasis. This is done, no doubt, to emphasize the significance of the statement, and He uses a form of teaching that should be copied by all. It makes the subject easier to remember and understand.

The phrase, *"For every one who asks receives,"* is a wide open, carte blanche statement that refers to everyone exactly as stated, that is, if we, in fact, do what verse 7 says.

Sometimes the asking, seeking, and knocking may take quite a period of time, even years.

If the request pertains to the plan of God or depends on the will of others, such may, in fact, take an involved period of time. However, many requests do not fall under that category and will be answered speedily. Nevertheless, the idea of these passages is that we are not to give up but to keep believing. We are not to let hindrances, obstacles, or difficulties deter us from that which we rightly seek. As well, I am sure the reader will understand that the very tenor of the words precludes frivolous requests.

FRIVOLITY

Regrettably, in the past few years, the deep and abiding intercession once practiced by some believers—which, in fact, ushered in tremendous moves of God, among other things—has been replaced, by and large, with frivolity. Too many modern Christians are taught the very opposite of what these passages demand. For instance, requests for bigger houses and bigger cars have replaced, at least for the most part, intercession for revival and the salvation of souls.

As well, most modern Christians are taught the "confession principle," which certainly has some validity but definitely not in the way it is presently taught. They are taught to ask one time and then begin to confess the answer into existence, irrespective as to what it might be. I might quickly add, irrespective, also, as to what the will of God might be.

THE WILL OF GOD

Such an attitude automatically assumes that it knows the will of God in any and all cases. In reality, there may be times that what we are asking is not the will of God, and the waiting period, as described in these passages, brings this out and shifts us to the direction desired by the Holy Spirit.

The idea that believers always know the will of God in any and all situations is preposterous indeed! Also, the very requirement of the child of God is to desire what Jesus said: *"Your will be done in earth, as it is heaven"* (Mat. 6:10).

PERSONAL

The phrase, *"And he who seeks finds,"* is a little different (as is the asking) than the statements made in verse 7.

Whereas verse 7 concerns itself more so with generalized terms, verse 8 makes the matter personal and, therefore, the guarantee of an even greater moment, if possible.

"And to him who knocks it shall be opened," once again takes it from the general realm to the personal position.

It is as if Christ is saying, "I personally guarantee you …."

Even as I dictate these words, I sense the presence of God.

What beautiful promises, and even more so, what a great and wonderful God we serve!

To be sure, on a personal basis, I have proven these promises over and over. And yet, there are some petitions of my own personal request that have not yet been answered. However, I know beyond the shadow of a doubt that they will be answered.

How do I know that? I know it because of what He has done in the past and because He has magnified His Word above all His name (Ps. 138:2).

VICTORY OVER SIN

The answer to the child of God in any and every capacity is Jesus Christ and Him crucified.

Because, for all practical purposes, the church has abandoned the Cross, most in the modern church world no longer even believe that what Jesus did at the Cross addresses the sin problem. So, they recommend humanistic psychology, which is actually of Satan. Even the most elementary Sunday school child ought to know that if the terrible sin problem, with all of its perversions and aberrations, can, in fact, be solved by the prattle of pitiful man, then Jesus needlessly came down here and died on a cruel Cross. The great problem in the modern church is unbelief and scriptural ignorance, but most of all, it's unbelief.

THE ROYAL TREASURY

"Or what man is there of you, whom if his son ask bread, will he give him a stone? Or if he asks a fish, will he give him a serpent?" (Mat. 7:9-10).

The antidote for care is to betake oneself to the royal treasury. Application there will meet with certain response, but the mode of application must follow the pattern as outlined in Matthew 6:9-13. There God's interests come first. They occur in a descending scale from Himself to His kingdom and from His kingdom to the earth.

The four human petitions occur in an ascending scale—from daily bread to final deliverance. The Lord does something in these two verses that is beautiful to behold: He lets the disciple know that God is not a machine but, in reality, a Father, albeit a heavenly Father. He is God, and as such, His thoughts and ways are not ours. Nevertheless, as is evidenced by His only Son, He has feelings, emotions, and passions, and will respond accordingly.

FEARS

Also, these two verses allay all fears that some have respecting relationship with the Lord. In fact, the entirety of verses 7 through 12 concerns relationship. Every word breathes with a parental concern and with sonship obligation.

Many believers have very little prayer life because they fear that the Lord will ask them to do something that is sorely displeasing to them. Both of these verses assure such a one that if his son ask bread, he will not be given a stone, or if he ask a fish, he will not instead be given a serpent.

The promise is inviolable.

Actually, it has a double meaning, which gives us a double security:

1.   It means that the Lord will give us what we ask and not substitute something else in its place.

2.   If, in fact, what we are asking is not God's will and will turn out to be a *"stone"* or *"serpent,"* He will guard us from receiving such. Also, during the time of waiting and consecration, He will show us what we truly need.

Tragically, all of us at one time or another may have asked for things that we truly thought we should have but would have turned out not to be the bread or fish we had first thought. However, in His sagacity, our heavenly Father instead steered us in another direction. Such is the reason for the delay sometimes experienced.

THE CROSS

We either believe that Jesus addressed every sin and in every manner at the Cross, or else, we don't believe. One cannot have it both ways. If we claim to believe that He, in fact, did address all sin at the Cross, then we know instinctively that man has no solution to this problem. So, for preachers to recommend humanistic psychology, it must mean that they have weighed the evidence, and in their own minds, they have come to a conclusion of unbelief that Calvary did not answer it all.

GOOD THINGS

"If you then, being evil, know how to give good gifts unto your children, how much more shall your Father which is in heaven give good things to them who ask Him?" (Mat. 7:11).

"If you then, being evil," refers to parents sometimes giving their children things that are not good for them as well as things that are good.

"Know how to give good gifts unto your children," portrays the efforts by fallen human nature to do the best for their children. The idea is that if some wicked fathers see to it that their children get what they ask and that they are fed, clothed, and protected, at least as far as is possible, then how much more will the heavenly Father do for His children who ask Him?

Luke adds to this wonderful scenario, *"Give the Holy Spirit to them who ask Him,"* which is meant to emphasize the gift that ultimately produces all others (Lk. 11:13).

The phrase, *"Good things,"* should include deliverance from dangers, preservation from evil, bodily healing and health, material prosperity, and any other answer to prayer, which are good things. As such, we should ask to receive them and no longer question the will of God in the matter. It is already His will, or this teaching of verses 7 through 11 is false.

However, the Lord allows Himself to interpret what these good things actually are. As well, the wise Christian will not only allow such but will insist upon it.

DO UNTO OTHERS AS YOU WOULD
HAVE THEM DO UNTO YOU

"Therefore all things whatsoever you would that men should do to you, do you even so to them; for this is the law and the prophets" (Mat. 7:12).

Verse 12 sums up the statutes and precepts of the kingdom; however, this Golden Rule does not authorize capricious benevolent action, but only what is reasonable and morally helpful and controlled by divine imitation (Mat. 5:48).

This principle of action and mode of life is, in fact, the sum of all Bible teaching. Jesus had a way of summing up extremely complex subjects into short statements that beautifully and wonderfully said what needed to be said!

"For this is the law and the prophets," proclaims in this one statement, which is commonly referred to as the Golden Rule, everything said in the Old Testament. It sums up the New Testament as well.

Inasmuch as our Lord has been dealing with the harsh judgmental spirit, He is now admonishing His followers to let the opposite feeling rule in their conduct toward others. Let all (the word *all* is emphatic) your dealings with men be conducted in the same spirit in which you would desire them to deal with you. In effect, the statement by Christ, in the summing up of the law—*"You shall love your neighbor as yourself"*—is essentially the same as this statement, but it provides the foundation of love, without which the Golden Rule cannot be done (Mat. 22:39-40).

THE STRAIT GATE

"Enter you in at the strait gate: for wide is the gate, and broad is the way, that leads to destruction, and many there be which go in thereat" (Mat. 7:13).

The entrance into the kingdom is declared the narrow gate of conversion, i.e., the acceptance of Christ as Saviour. The Lord adds that precious few take the opportunity to pass in by it.

This double statement, as given in both verses 13 and 14, is offensive to the moralist, for it declares him to be as hopelessly corrupt as the vilest, and, thereby, he needs a moral re-creation. It states that few are thus reborn.

The phrase, *"Enter you in at the strait gate,"* proclaims that the process of conversion must take place in order to be saved. *"The strait gate"* is the door, who is Jesus (Jn. 10:1).

The word *strait* also refers to being narrow. Consequently, that means only one way, which excludes all other ways. That way, i.e. gate, is the Bible. That excludes all religions as well as the part of Christianity that is corrupt.

THE WAYS OF THE WORLD

Humanistic psychology cannot show one single individual anywhere at anytime that it has set free.

So, for preachers to believe this wisdom of the world, which is earthly, sensual, and devilish (James 3:15), simply says that they do not believe the *"wisdom of God,"* which is the Cross of Christ (I Cor. 1:21).

Unbelief is the most dangerous place and position of all in that the bottom line is that men simply do not believe that Jesus Christ *"is the propitiation for our sins: and not for ours only, but also for the sins of the whole world"* (I Jn. 2:2).

CULTURE

It is sad that sometime back, a group of religious leaders in America signed a concordance stating that no effort would be made to convert Catholics because, as they stated it, Catholics are already saved. These religious leaders were from every religious background, including Pentecostals and charismatics. Regrettably, they knew little of the Word of God, or they would not have signed such a paper. Catholics are not saved. It's true that some Catholics do give their hearts to Christ; however, with that being the case, if they want to maintain their walk with the Lord, they're going to have to get out of the Catholic Church. One cannot embrace false doctrine, at least to the extent that Catholic doctrine is false (and it is altogether false), and maintain his walk with God. As someone has well said, if you put a live chicken under a dead hen, you're going to conclude with two dead chickens.

A lady asked me one time why we were carrying out mission works in foreign countries, such as, among other things, the airing of our telecast. She claimed that by doing so, we were affecting their culture and meddling with their religion, with which they were evidently satisfied.

It is difficult to understand how someone who called herself a Christian could come up with such foolishness. Evidently, the woman knew absolutely nothing about the Bible.

Most definitely the gospel will affect anyone's culture, which is, I might quickly add, demented, as is all culture; however, its affectation of such culture will be for the better, I might also quickly add. All of the culture in the world, including American culture, is corrupt, evil, wicked, etc. Of course, some cultures are worse than others, but all are labeled evil by the Lord (Rom., Chpt. 3).

BIBLE CULTURE

Irrespective of the color of one's skin, the country in which one has lived, or what type of culture one has previously engaged, whenever the believing sinner comes to Christ, he changes. In fact, everything changes. When a person comes to Christ, he enters into Bible culture, which means he forsakes all of the old culture that he had.

The truth is, the gospel of Jesus Christ and Him crucified affects all culture, and does so in a positive way.

Whether people the world over are satisfied with their religion or not is of little consequence. The truth is, "their religion" is of Satan and will cause their souls to be eternally lost. This is the very reason for the command of Christ, *"Go ye into all the world, and preach the gospel to every creature"* (Mk. 16:15).

DESTRUCTION

As we have stated, the phrase, *"For wide is the gate, and broad is the way, that leads to destruction,"* proclaims the many and varied religions of the world that are false and will lead to eternal hellfire. I know that is blunt, but it happens to be true.

These evil ways are broad, which speaks, as well, of being very enticing and alluring. As such, most fall easily into its maw.

By contrast the *"strait gate,"* or door, is narrow, which means that most often one must search to find it.

These passages completely refute the fallacious idea that approach to God is like the many spokes of a wheel, with all leading to the same hub.

No! Christians and Muslims most definitely do not pray to the same God, and the list goes on. Allah is a name chosen by Muhammad from one of the many gods of the Babylonians. In fact, no man can reach God the Father except through Jesus Christ, who is the door, and I might quickly add, the only door (Jn. 10:1; 14:6).

To be sure, preachers who espouse the narrow way are called narrow themselves. As such, we are hated, reviled, laughed at, lampooned, and most, if not all of the time, ostracized.

MOST ARE ETERNALLY LOST

"And many there be which go in thereat," refers to most of the world and for all time!

Tragically, many, if not most, of these people thought they were saved, ready, prepared, or any other terminology that one may apply to the subject.

However, these who entered this wide gate were not saved. There is nothing in the world worse than a false way of salvation! Tragically, and as Christ said, *"Many there be which go in thereat."*

REQUIREMENTS

"Because strait is the gate, and narrow is the way, which leads unto life, and few there be who find it" (Mat. 7:14).

Every contrite heart earnestly desires to be among the *"few."*

"Because strait is the gate," means that the requirements are greater than most are willing to accept. At the outset, much determination is required, and afterward, much self-denial.

Men do not enter this strait gate because they cannot carry their sins with them, and they love their sins.

However, what they do not realize is that whatever the Lord takes away is always that which is harming us, no matter how enjoyable at the present it may seem to be. Then He always gives us something far greater to take its place.

Religion can only take away; it can add nothing. As an aside, religion is something that is devised by man, which means it's not devised by God, and it claims to help one in some way, which can never be accepted by God. Bible Christianity is not a religion. It is, in fact, a relationship, and that relationship is with a man—the man Christ Jesus. In fact, God cannot use anything that originates with man. If it is used by God, whatever it might be, it must be conceived by the Holy Spirit, birthed by the Holy Spirit, orchestrated by the Holy Spirit, and carried out in totality by the Holy Spirit. While the Lord uses men and women, that doesn't mean they conceive the idea, whatever it might be.

Religion can only take away; it can add nothing, at least nothing that is good. However, even though taking away, Jesus then gives eternal life with all of its attendant joys, developments, and fulfillments.

In other words, that which He takes away from us—our sins and self-will—even though at times seeming attractive, can, in reality, do nothing but hurt. Sadly, many people have to come to a place of great hurt before they will finally say yes to Christ.

NARROW IS THE WAY

"And narrow is the way," means exactly what it says. However, it is narrow only in the sense of the things of this world and definitely not in the sense of the things of God.

The world's system is the enemy of the believer, and that means everything in it, with the exception of the narrow way carved out by the Lord.

Admittedly, many preachers, churches, and even entire religious denominations have attempted to broaden the way, but they only succeed in destroying it. This way is His way, and as such, must not be tampered with by man.

This means that the believer should be very careful as to what he reads, where he goes, friends with whom he associates, business ventures into which he enters, and even the thoughts he thinks. Is this restrictive?

It definitely is restrictive as far as the world is concerned; however, the true child of God has no interest in the world, so rather than be restrictive to him, it has the opposite effect.

RESTRICTIONS

Such restrictions enable him to draw closer to the Lord, who expands every legitimate horizon in a manner that the world could never even begin to approach.

"Which leads unto life," bears out exactly what I have just said.

Actually, even though speaking of eternal life, Christ was mostly referring to the present in the fullest nature—life as *the fulfillment of the highest idea of being.*

Actually, without Jesus, there is no life! Only in Jesus can one truly find the meaning of life (Jn. 14:6). Please note the following diagram:

- The only way to God is through Jesus Christ (Jn. 14:6).

- The only way to Christ is by the means of the Cross (I Cor. 2:2).

- The only way to the Cross is by a denial of self (Lk. 9:23).

This means that without Jesus, the richest man in the world doesn't know what life means. It also means that the most educated man in the world doesn't know what life is unless he has Christ. That is the reason Jesus said, *"That they might have life, and that they might have it more abundantly"* (Jn. 10:10).

Consequently, this life is not a religion, philosophy, or church, but instead, a person—the man Christ Jesus.

FEW THERE BE WHO FIND IT

"And few there be who find it" speaks of this life, which Jesus addresses. The words *"find it,"* actually mean that some do search, at least for a little while, and then give up.

Also, the phrase means that this strait gate and narrow way are not easily found.

The reason for that is the deception used by Satan that throws people onto another track, which, in effect, leads to destruction. Satan is a master at this procedure, and inasmuch as the fall of man in the garden of Eden was brought about by deception, man continues to be easily deceived.

However, if one truly seeks, one will truly find (v. 8).

Naught have I gotten but what I received;
Grace has bestowed it since I have believed;
Boasting excluded, pride I abase;
I'm only a believer saved by grace!

Once I was foolish, and sin ruled my heart,
Causing my footsteps from God to depart;
Jesus has found me, happy my case;
I now am a believer saved by grace!

Tears unavailing, no merit had I;
Mercy had saved me, or else I must die;
Sin had alarmed me, fearing God's face;
But now I'm a believer saved by grace!

Suffer a sinner whose heart overflows,
Loving his Saviour to tell what he knows;
Once more to tell it would I embrace—
I'm only a believer saved by grace!

THE SERMON *on the* MOUNT

FALSE PROPHETS

FALSE PROPHETS

"BEWARE OF FALSE PROPHETS, who come to you in sheep's clothing, but inwardly they are ravening wolves" (Mat. 7:15).

BEWARE OF FALSE PROPHETS

The preachers of falsehood are now introduced because they deny the need of Christ, they attempt to add something to Christ, or else, they "use" Christ to promote some man-made philosophy.

The fact is, due to having almost no knowledge of the Cross of Christ respecting sanctification, most Christians are living lives of spiritual failure. Regrettably, much of the charismatic world completely denies the Cross of Christ, claiming that it was the worst defeat in human history. Consequently, they say that the Cross, the blood, etc., should never be mentioned. Pure and simple, this is another gospel, fostered by another spirit, presenting another Jesus (II Cor. 11:4).

The phrase, *"Beware of false prophets,"* is said in the sternest of measures! This means that there definitely will be false prophets, and the truth is, there are far more false prophets than there are true prophets. Those who are false are at least one of, if not Satan's greatest, weapons.

If one is to notice, Christ did not refer to false teachers as Peter did (II Pet. 2:1), which refers to persons falsely interpreting fundamental truths, but instead, He mentioned false prophets. These falsely claimed to bring messages directly from God. They claimed to bring from God the true message of salvation, but their claim was false. Regrettably, millions have followed, and do follow, these false prophets.

HOW DO WE RECOGNIZE FALSE PROPHETS?

That's a good question!

One could fill up this book with the answer to that question, or one can answer it with a few words. The conclusion would probably be about the same in either case.

The prophet who preaches something other than Christ and Him crucified, in other words, the Cross of Christ is not his message, must be labeled as "false," no matter what he claims. Paul addressed this by saying:

I marvel that you are so soon removed from Him (the Holy Spirit) *who called you into the grace of Christ* (made possible by the Cross) *unto another gospel* (anything which doesn't have the Cross as its object of faith): *Which is not another* (presents the fact that Satan's aim is not so much to deny the gospel, which he can little do, as to corrupt it); *but there be some who trouble you, and would pervert the gospel of Christ* (once again, to make the object of faith something other than the Cross).

ACCURSED

But though we (Paul and his associates), *or an angel from heaven, preach any other gospel unto you than that which we have preached unto you* (Jesus Christ and Him crucified), *let him be accursed* (eternally condemned; the Holy Spirit speaks this through Paul, making this very serious). *As we said before, so say I now again* (at some time past, he had said the same thing to them, making their defection even more serious), *If any man preach any other gospel unto you* (anything other than the Cross) *than that you have received* (which saved your souls), *let him be accursed* ('eternally condemned,' which means the loss of the soul). *For do I now persuade men, or God?* (In essence, Paul is saying, 'Do I preach man's doctrine, or God's?') *or do I seek to please men?* (This is what false apostles do.) *for if I yet pleased men, I should not be the servant of Christ* (one cannot please both men and God at the same time) (Gal. 1:6-10) (The Expositor's Study Bible).

SHEEP'S CLOTHING

The phrase, *"Who come to you in sheep's clothing,"* of course, speaks of false prophets and proclaims their deception.

They have on the clothing of sheep, and as a result, they look like the real thing. As well, *"sheep's clothing"* denotes their false humility, gentle ways, and soothing mannerisms, all designed to deceive. Paul had something to say about this as well. He said:

> *For such are false apostles, deceitful workers* (they have no rightful claim to the apostolic office; they are deceivers), *transforming themselves into the apostles of Christ.* (They have called themselves to this office.) *And no marvel* (true believers should not be surprised); *for Satan himself is transformed into an angel of light.* (This means he pretends to be that which he is not.) *Therefore it is no great thing if his ministers* (Satan's ministers) *also be transformed as the ministers of righteousness* (despite their claims, they were 'Satan's ministers' because they preached something other than the Cross [I Cor. 1:17-18, 21, 23; 2:2; Gal. 1:8-9]); *whose end shall be according to their works* (that 'end' is spiritual destruction [Phil. 3:18-19]) (II Cor. 11:13-15) (The Expositor's Study Bible).

RAVENING WOLVES

The phrase, *"But inwardly they are ravening wolves,"* proclaims that the outward is not nearly as obvious as the inward. Sadly, most are fooled by the outward, i.e., sheep's clothing.

In truth, and as is obvious, the nature of a wolf is the opposite of sheep.

The meaning of *"ravening"* pertains to violence and greed. This means that their message is designed but for one purpose, and that is to oppose the truth and injure the ones whom they are addressing. They do so for their own personal gain.

These false prophets could possibly be said to fall into two categories. They are:

1. DECEPTION

These proclaimers of a false gospel actually think they are preaching the truth but, in reality, are deceived themselves. As such, they do not know the Lord, and even though carrying the trappings of profession outwardly, they have never been changed. No matter how cultured or cultivated, because of not truly knowing Christ even though professing Him, inwardly, they are *"ravening wolves."*

These could fall into many areas of corrupt Christianity. As such, they do not preach the truth because they do not know the truth. They preach a lie pure and simple, and those who are deceived, which numbers into the multiple millions, will be eternally lost!

2. A LUST FOR MONEY

The second category of these false prophets has at its core a lust for money. Consequently, they take one of two approaches, or a combination of both.

The first category consists of those who are in the ministry for intellectual, personal, or monetary reasons. They are not called of God. They are *"hirelings"* pure and simple. They preach what their congregations want to hear instead of what they need to hear, i.e., the Word of God. This pretty much describes the seeker sensitive churches.

THE MONEY MESSAGE

The promoters of the money message use Christ to promote this philosophy. Much, if not most, of their message is tailored, designed, and directed in a manner to get people to give money. It is done under the guise of faith or gargantuan returns. In other words, it's a quick way to get rich; however, the only ones who get rich are the preachers. It is a vain philosophy pure and simple.

In fact, their philosophy is subtly presented, with much of the trappings of the true gospel around it. This makes it extremely easy to believe and is deceptive because it appeals to the base nature of man, even Christian man, who desires to be rich. All of it is done under a cloak of the blessings of God, etc. It is easy to believe simply because God most definitely does bless His people abundantly so. I personally believe that according to the Word of the Lord, He will prosper any believer who looks to Him exclusively. So, there is a lot of truth in what these particular preachers say, and it is the truth that serves as the bait. However, as previously stated, the real truth is the only ones who are getting rich in this particular type of so-called gospel are the preachers.

THE SHOWCASE

Consequently, this "gospel" is showcased by the make of car they drive, the cut of their clothes, the type of house in which they live, and the amount of money they have. If one is to notice, all of these things are externals, which appeals to the self-life and, in truth, must be crucified in Christ before one can truly know the will of God.

Believers should give to the Lord, which refers to His work. However, they must make certain that that to which they are giving is, in truth, the work of God.

Regrettably, most money that goes for what purports to be the work of God is just another scam. Let's put it another way: If the preacher you are supporting is not preaching the Cross of Christ, at least for salvation, any support given to such will be wasted. In effect, such giving supports Satan's ministers.

SUPPOSING THAT GAIN IS GODLINESS

Once again, the apostle Paul addressed this very question, which I call the "money gospel." He said:

Perverse disputings of men of corrupt minds, and destitute of the truth, supposing that gain is godliness: from such withdraw yourself.

He went on to say,

But godliness with contentment is great gain. For we brought nothing into this world, and it is certain we can carry nothing out. And having food and raiment let us be therewith content. But they who will be rich fall into temptation and a snare, and into many foolish and hurtful lusts, which drown men in destruction and perdition. For the love of money is the root of all evil: which while some coveted after, they have erred from the faith, and pierced themselves through with many sorrows (I Tim. 6:5-10).

The great apostle then said, *"But you, O man of God, flee these things; and follow after righteousness, godliness, faith, love, patience, meekness"* (I Tim. 6:11).

Need I say more?

FRUIT

"You shall know them by their fruits. Do men gather grapes of thorns, or figs of thistles?" (Mat. 7:16).

A proper understanding of the Cross and faith in that finished work of Christ presents the only means of overcoming sin. There is no other sacrifice for sin! So, if the believer doesn't know or understand this all-important truth, then irrespective of how sincere the believer might be, in one way or the other, such a believer is going to live a life of spiritual failure. While such a person is definitely saved, that is, if his faith continues to be in Christ, at the same time, he definitely isn't victorious (Rom. 7:15).

The phrase, *"You shall know them by their fruits,"* is meant to express that the appearance and claims of these false prophets are no proof of their true character. Claims and prophecies abound, which have no validity and, in fact, do not come to pass.

The question, *"Do men gather grapes of thorns, or figs of thistles?"* does not ask, Do thorns produce grapes? etc., because men automatically know that such does not produce grapes or figs.

So Jesus is telling His followers to use the same common sense in spiritual matters as they show in matters of everyday life.

What a blessing if all Christians did this!

A PERSONAL EXPERIENCE

I am amazed at some Christian businessmen who will go to meticulous lengths to check the validity of claims made by certain products, etc. And yet, those same businessmen at times will accept the wild extravagant claims of some preachers without checking into it. Jesus is saying that they should use as much sense with the one as with the other!

Years ago, a businessman, who, in fact, gave large sums of money to the work of God, came to me speaking of a particular preacher whom he was planning to sponsor, which involved quite a sum of money.

I was not acquainted with the preacher but strongly urged him to check out the matter.

I said to him, "Sadly and regrettably, many of the claims made by many preachers simply will not hold water, so to speak. In other words, it is not true."

He told me how he certainly believed what this man said, even though he had no proof of what was being said.

THE RESULTS

About three months later, he came to me, very distraught I might add.

He said, "I had occasion to visit the place where my money was supposed to be spent building a certain project and, in fact, there was no project there, and nothing was being planned."

He then said, "I threw my money away!"

Yes he did, which meant that it could have been used for a legitimate work of God, but instead, it was not only wasted, but it supported a false prophet.

Sometime back, one of our supporters—a man, I might quickly add, who had given strongly to our work and ministry—spoke of going overseas and seeing firsthand the work of our child care ministry in Africa. I strongly encouraged him to do so, which he did.

After having stayed for nearly two weeks, when he came back, he said, "Brother Swaggart, if you could get all of your supporters to see this work and exactly how much good it is doing, you wouldn't have to plead for funds any longer!"

He has been back several times since.

OF WHAT TYPE OF FRUIT IS JESUS SPEAKING?

The true gospel of Jesus Christ will always be the foundation of good fruit. Of course, every preacher claims to be preaching the true gospel when, in fact, many, if not most, are not.

However, irrespective of the good intentions, if the gospel is not being proclaimed as it should be, whatever else is being done will be inconsequential as well. The fruit will be souls saved, believers baptized with the Holy Spirit, sick bodies healed, and lives changed, which develops righteousness (I Tim. 6:11).

Regrettably, wild extravagant claims are made all the time of great numbers being saved, etc. However, some of these claims are spurious, with very precious few of these people being found.

Once again, claims are one thing while the actual fruit is something else altogether. Before anything is supported, it ought to be diligently checked into.

In the last few years, such claims of healings and miracles have been bandied about as if commonplace. In fact, some few are true and for that we are thankful. However, sadly, most are spurious.

A PERSONAL EXPERIENCE

Sometime back, I had the occasion to visit briefly with a man about this very subject. I did not at all agree with his hypothesis, but still, I could not deny his findings.

Claiming to be of sincere heart (which I hope he was) regarding a particular evangelist, he "checked out" several of the proposed outstanding healings.

He said to me, "Brother Swaggart, I simply wanted to find that which was genuine, but there was no way that anyone could conclude, at least honestly, that anything of a physical nature had changed in these particular people."

The truth is that the Lord still heals the sick and performs miracles. He answers prayers and still does great and mighty things. However, false claims in no way glorify God because nowhere in the Bible does one find God placing a premium on dishonesty.

Regrettably, it seems that much money in Christian giving goes more so to wild extravagant claims than to the actual fruit. This proclaims that many Christians are not truthfully heeding the admonitions of Christ if, in fact, they know them at all.

The true gospel will produce righteousness in the life of the believer. Peter said, *"As obedient children, not fashioning yourselves according to the former lusts in your ignorance: But as He who has called you is holy, so you be holy in all manner of conversation"* (I Pet. 1:14-15). The word *conversation*, as then used, actually means "lifestyle."

GOOD FRUIT

"Even so every good tree brings forth good fruit; but a corrupt tree brings forth evil fruit" (Mat. 7:17).

The phrase, *"Even so every good tree brings forth good fruit,"* should be the obvious conclusion of all. Therefore, allow us to say it again: Every Christian ought to be a fruit inspector, and diligently so!

Regrettably, there aren't a whole lot of good trees around. As a result, there isn't a whole lot of good fruit.

Modern Christendom has been amazingly influenced by the hype of Hollywood and the ad agencies. In fact, the hype is so bad that it is very difficult anymore to know the truth unless it is minutely inspected. As good fruit is the single most important thing in the world, every Christian should be diligent in their inspection. To heed reports of biased individuals, whether pro or con, is unwise indeed. Regrettably, this is the course that most

Christians follow. They simply do not inspect for themselves, at least for the most part. Consequently, probably one could say without exaggeration that the far greater majority support a corrupt tree bringing forth evil fruit.

THE CROSS

If the believer doesn't understand the Cross of Christ as it regards sanctification—in other words, how we live for God, how we order our behavior, how we have victory over the world, the flesh, and the Devil, and how we grow in grace and the joy of the Lord—such a believer is very apt to follow bad fruit. Pride functions graphically so in such an atmosphere.

There are sins of passion and there are sins of pride. Sins of passion, which are works of the flesh (Gal. 5:19-21), are very obvious, while sins of pride are not so very obvious. Sins of passion include all the vices and, of course, are very evil.

Sins of pride function in another category altogether and are not at all easy to detect. Self-righteousness would probably be the best explanation.

Without exception, any belief system other than the Cross of Calvary ultimately leads to self-righteousness.

FALSE PROPHETS

One of, if not the greatest, hindrances in the early church was these false prophets. They hindered Paul greatly by denigrating his character, by claiming to have a deeper revelation, or by making outright false claims. Many of Paul's epistles were written to refute the error they brought into the early church. In fact, Paul had planted the church at Corinth, with almost all of the converts having come to Christ through his ministry. Nevertheless, they came very close to turning on Paul simply because the Corinthians were lax in checking out the fruit. II Corinthians, Chapter 7, proclaims their repentance, which greatly gladdened the heart of Paul, as would be obvious.

He was strong in his denunciation of these individuals, calling them *"false apostles, deceitful workers, transforming themselves into the apostles of Christ."*

He then went on to say that they were, in effect, Satan's ministers (II Cor. 11:13-15).

When the Corinthians who had been saved under his ministry demanded his (Paul's) credentials because they had been corrupted by these false apostles, he told them, *"You are our epistle* (fruit) *written in our hearts, known and read of all men"* (II Cor. 3:2). The greatest fruit of all was their conversion, which they were too blind to see.

He brought forth good fruit, while these false apostles brought forth evil fruit.

WHAT IS EVIL FRUIT?

It is a false gospel.

The evil fruit is greed, selfishness, and self-will generated by this false gospel, which is the opposite of righteousness. To be frank, it is very easy to look at the product of most churches and determine what kind of gospel is being preached by the fruit it produces.

Most churches, and I exaggerate not, are filled with people whose lives have never been changed. They do the same things, act in the same manner, and conduct themselves in the same way as those who profess nothing. No, one is not talking about sinless perfection, for that, in fact, does not exist.

As well, one is not speaking of incidents, which will affect even the most righteous at one time or the other, that demand repentance and forgiveness. We are speaking of the overall lifestyle that has experienced no change.

If people associate themselves with a church of any kind, most claim to be saved. While it is certainly true that some are, still, if one looks at all the churches in the aggregate, most are not saved and actually produce evil fruit.

Truthfully, many churches are filled with moralists. These individuals attempt to live by a set of rules (which they break as often as not) and think by these rules, they are saved.

They think that good morals, which, in reality, are not so good at all, constitute salvation. They have never really made Christ their Saviour. Many may have made a mental affirmation but really did not experience a changed heart. As such, they continue to produce evil fruit, even though it is of the moral type, which, in fact, is a man-devised morality that God will not accept.

To be sure, good morality is definitely important; however, it must be the morality effected by Christ and not that devised by men.

THE GOOD TREE AND THE CORRUPT TREE

"A good tree cannot bring forth evil fruit, neither can a corrupt tree bring forth good fruit" (Mat. 7:18).

The phrase, *"A good tree cannot bring forth evil fruit,"* is strong indeed.

It means that no matter the storms or vicissitudes of life that affect this good tree, it will continue to bear good fruit. Regrettably, even though it is a good tree, and despite it continuing to bear good fruit, storms or problems of one kind or the other cause many believers to turn away. The sadness is that there are so few good trees that often such believers turn to a corrupt tree, which cannot bring forth good fruit.

As well, it should be hastily said that if it is a good tree, all the people in the world saying otherwise will not make it any less good. Approval or disapproval on the part of people changes nothing. The Lord is the one who owns the good tree. While it is true that He may have to purge it and, no doubt, will, still, such is done only that it may *"bring forth more fruit"* (Jn. 15:2).

However, the purging process is not pretty to behold because it constitutes the dying of certain things, and no one likes to watch something die. It is not pleasant, and most turn away, even the best of Christians. What they think is destruction is oftentimes the very opposite!

To the contrary, it does no good to purge a corrupt tree because it is corrupt not in just some individual branches, but, in fact, it is corrupt down to the very roots.

CUT IT DOWN

"Every tree that brings not forth good fruit is hewn down, and cast into the fire" (Mat. 7:19).

As just stated, this corrupt tree will lose far more than just unproductive branches, but in truth, it will be cut down entirely.

This is that of which John the Baptist was speaking in his ministry that introduced Christ. He said *"And now also the axe is laid unto the root of the trees: therefore every tree which brings not forth good fruit is hewn down, and cast into the fire"* (Mat. 3:10).

In fact, at that time, he was speaking of Israel, which was totally cut down in AD 70 because of their rejection of Christ.

It should be understood that if the Lord would do an entire nation this way, especially those who were called His chosen, would He certainly not do the same to individual false prophets?

Even as the good fruit is proof positive, still, the durability of the good tree, despite the storms, etc., means that it will continue to bear good fruit.

RECOGNITION

"Wherefore by their fruits you shall know them" (Mat. 7:20).

The Lord concludes His statement on false prophets by telling Christians to be fruit inspectors. Once again, He is talking about fruit and not hype.

If one is to notice, Christ did *not* say:

- "By the good recommendation of others, you shall know them."

- "Because major religious denominations approve of them."

- "Because they are popular."

- "Everybody likes them," etc.

In fact, almost none of the above will be true if they are truly bearing good fruit. One is to inspect the fruit and not the things just mentioned.

In truth, not a single religious leader, except two members of the Sanhedrin, approved of Christ. Actually, they disapproved of Him so much that they killed Him. As well, despite the greatest miracles the world had ever known, and despite the fact that Jesus Christ was perfect in every respect—in conduct, in attitude, in personality, in appearance, etc.—His crowds greatly thinned in the last year of His public ministry because His popularity had greatly waned due to the opposition of the religious leaders (Jn. 6:66-67).

However, He was known by the fruits He produced in changed lives, great miracles of healing, and above all, the presentation of the gospel by His great sacrifice at Calvary.

Therefore, if the people were going to know Him by the well wishes of the religious leaders, they would have rejected Him out of hand as, in fact, most did.

NOT EVERYONE WHO SAYS ...

"Not every one who says unto Me, Lord, Lord, shall enter into the kingdom of heaven; but he who does the will of my Father who is in heaven" (Mat. 7:21).

The phrase, *"Not every one who says unto Me, Lord, Lord,"* is wide in its sweeping statement!

First of all, these individuals, whomever they may have been, claimed to recognize Christ as Lord. However, their claim was bogus, or else, they had only mentally affirmed their recognition of Christ without actually experiencing true conversion.

As well, the repetition of the word *Lord* expresses astonishment as if to say, "Are we to be disowned?"

This one Scripture proclaims the fact that many *profess* but do not actually *possess*. In truth, and according to the *"few there be who find it"* in verse 14, most fall into this saddened category.

The phrase, *"Shall enter into the kingdom of heaven,"* means to be truly converted and, thereby, at least in a spiritual sense, have already entered into this kingdom.

THE WILL OF MY FATHER

"But he who does the will of My Father who is in heaven," refers to those who also say, *"Lord, Lord,"* but, in fact, have been truly saved and have entered into a family relationship with Christ.

So, all the professors and the possessors say, *"Lord, Lord,"* but the truth is here illustrated that a mere confession without corresponding results in the heart is not enough. Regrettably, this adversely affects the far greater majority of those who call themselves Christians.

What is the will of the Father?

Verse 24 tells us what the *"will of My Father"* is: *"Therefore whosoever hears these sayings of Mine, and does them."*

In other words, the Word of God is the criterion and the measuring rod, which will always correspond with Christ as He is the living Word. This means that He and the written Word are indivisible.

This one verse of Scripture is going to keep many, if not most, out of the kingdom.

THE YARDSTICK

"Many will say to me in that day, Lord, Lord, have we not prophesied in Your name? and in Your name have cast out devils (demons)? *and in Your name done many wonderful works?"* (Mat. 7:22).

Many have stumbled over verse 22, not actually understanding it, but its meaning is clear.

Miracles and prophecies can truly be of God, but at the same time, can truly be of Satan. Jesus later said, *"For there shall arise false Christs, and false prophets, and shall show great signs and wonders; insomuch that, if it were possible, they shall deceive the very elect"* (Mat. 24:24).

Therefore, the admonition is clear that such, even if performed by a true prophet of the Lord, should not and, in fact, must not be the yardstick by which such is judged. The Word of God alone is to be the judge of doctrine.

It is regrettable that too many Pentecostals (of which I am one) and Charismatics put entirely too much credit in these things, as helpful and violable as they may be, and are, therefore, led astray by wild claims and exaggerations.

It should be pointed out, as well, that even though these things were done or claimed to be "in His name," still, this within itself also was no validity. Actually, the criterion is simple: Everything we believe must be based on Christ and the Cross, which will then be based on the Word.

God's solution for dying humanity is Jesus Christ and Him crucified. In fact, that's what it always has been, what it is now, and what it ever shall be.

THE WILL OF GOD AND THE WILL OF MAN

One might say that most every preacher in the world, at least in Christianity, does what he does *"in His name."* However, miracles performed and prophecies given, along with the ready use of His name, prove nothing. It is abiding by the Word of God that is always the acid test. If the Cross of Christ is not the foundation, then it is a sure sign that individuals are not interpreting the Word correctly, or else, are denying it altogether.

As we have already stated, miracles performed and prophecies given, along with the ready use of His name, prove nothing. These things, although scriptural, will not cover the disregarded balance of the Word of God.

In this scenario, and according to verse 21, the will of man and the will of the Father are placed side by side. One cannot have man's will, whether his or others, and God's will at the same time. So, the will of God is the criterion, which is the Word of God in its entirety.

FALSE TEACHERS

"And then will I profess unto them, I never knew you: depart from me, you who work iniquity" (Mat. 7:23).

Any direction by the believer other than the Cross of Christ always and without exception leads to self-righteousness. Just because a so-called believer is not mixed up in one of the vices (whatever that might be) doesn't mean he is living a life of victory over sin.

In fact, there are millions of so-called Christians whom the world thinks are very moral but, in reality, are trusting in their own self-righteousness instead of the righteousness of God. This latter refers to faith in what Christ did for us at the Cross.

Verse 23 tells us that false teachers are workers of iniquity, however attractive their personal character may be. This judgment is today called narrow, unchristian, violent, and bigoted, but it is the Master's judgment and, therefore, perfect.

The moral fruit of these false teachers is corruption in the church and in the world, so how can such produce changed lives?

The phrase, *"And then will I profess unto them,"* proclaims a coming day of reckoning, which we all should heed very carefully!

This will be at the *"great white throne judgment"* and will be professed openly in the face of all men (Rev. 20:11-15).

The phrase, *"I never knew you,"* means that even while all this religious activity was taking place, there was, in fact, no personal relationship with Christ. It was all profession and the use of His name without really knowing who the person was who carried the name. Please notice the following:

- The only way, and I mean the only way, to God is through Jesus Christ (Jn. 14:6).

- The only way to Jesus Christ is by and through the Cross (Lk. 9:23).

- The only way to the Cross is a denial of self (Lk. 14:26-27).

THE NAME OF JESUS

The name of Jesus can be used to gain riches, place and position, and the accolades of men, at least in some circles. Therefore, it was used, but it was without any relationship with Him personally, and also, it was not by their abiding by all of His Word.

If the Cross of Christ is ignored, which it is in most circles, this fully means that one is not abiding by His Word (Rom. 6:1-14; 8:1-11; I Cor. 1:17-18, 23; 2:2; Col. 2:10-15).

The phrase, *"Depart from Me, you who work iniquity,"* is chilling indeed!

Depart where?

John said, *"And whosoever was not found written in the Book of Life was cast into the lake of fire"* (Rev. 20:15). It should be readily understood that that of which John is speaking here is not merely the loss of reward but the loss of one's soul.

INIQUITY

As well, the word *iniquity* is not speaking of sin generally because every Christian is troubled in some way by fault and failure. This type of iniquity refers to those who were attempting to serve two masters as described in verses 22 through 24.

Their eye (spirit) was evil, and consequently, the light that went into them was darkness, and *"how great is that darkness!"*

As previously stated in commentary on those verses, this meant that such are so spiritually twisted, despite the miracles and the use of His name, that whatever light of the gospel that went into them, it was immediately turned to darkness.

In other words, they twisted the Scripture to make it mean something they desired instead of what it actually meant.

A FALSE WAY

It speaks of a false way, a wrong direction, and a wrong-headedness, which meant these false prophets earnestly worked at this false way.

I have heard preachers do this—find a Scripture that they could twist in order to cause people to give money—with that only in mind.

I have heard preachers twist the Scripture, as well, concerning the baptism with the Holy Spirit, which they had denied. Therefore, the light that went into them was turned to darkness. Many times I have heard preachers twist the Scripture as it regards the Cross of Christ, trying to make it mean something other than what it was originally intended. Sorrowfully, millions are in the religion business, but they really do not know Jesus as Saviour. Sadder still, this fact will one day be exclaimed before all.

THE SAYINGS OF CHRIST

"Therefore whosoever hears these sayings of Mine, and does them, I will liken him unto a wise man, who built his house upon a rock" (Mat. 7:24).

The phrase, *"Therefore whosoever hears these sayings of Mine, and does them,"* characterizes in very simple words that which it will take to have eternal life.

The implication is that many, if not most, hear His sayings but do not do them. Consequently, salvation is pronounced in two directives: hearing and doing.

This lays to rest the fallacious doctrine that one can claim to have believed Christ and, therefore, has been saved, and then continue to practice sin as, in fact, multiple millions do!

Some claim that the only difference in the believer and the unbeliever is the shed blood of Jesus Christ having been applied to the heart and life of the believer. They claim that the believer sins just as the unbeliever, etc.

While it is certainly true that the blood of Jesus Christ having been applied by faith to the believer's heart and life is the beginning of the great salvation process, still, if it has truly been applied, a changed life will be the result. It will be a change so remarkable, in fact, that it will be obvious to all.

A NEW CREATION

In other words, the drunk quits drinking, the thief quits stealing, the liar quits lying, and the immoral cease their immoral activities.

In truth, Paul said, *"Therefore if any man be in Christ, he is a new creature: old things are passed away; behold, all things are become new"* (II Cor. 5:17).

If this does not happen in the life of an individual, it is a sure sign that the individual has not truly believed with his heart but, in fact, has only proclaimed a mental affirmation, which is not acceptable to the Lord, and of which these passages speak.

However, truly being born again and becoming a new creature in Christ Jesus does not mean sinless perfection. While struggles with certain things may continue, still, the change that is produced will be obvious to all, and grace will be given to further subdue every unholy trait.

THE ROCK

The phrase, *"I will liken him unto a wise man, who built his house upon a rock,"* now proclaims that which will actually stand the acid test. The area where Jesus was speaking contained rock very near the surface and sometimes even on the surface. Therefore, there was no excuse for not providing the suitable foundation for the house of salvation.

The only reason that one could not find a suitable place, especially with such places obvious, was because of self-will. Too many individuals want salvation, but they desire their own will at the same time. Such is not to be.

When Jesus died on Calvary, He died to save us not only from sin but also from the very receptacle of that sin, self-will.

Once again, the criterion is obedience to the Word of God. If one knows and obeys the Word, this and this alone is constituted as the rock. A house built on anything else—no matter how acceptable to the world and no matter how much approved by men—will not stand. This means that all the religions of the world, along with all false doctrine perpetrated by false prophets, will ultimately come crashing down. It may be in this life, or it may be in the judgment to come, but whichever, it will be found wanting.

THE ATTACK OF SATAN

"And the rain descended, and the floods came, and the winds blew, and beat upon that house; and it fell not; for it was founded upon a rock" (Mat. 7:25).

First of all, we must understand that the only thing standing between man and eternal hell is the Cross of Christ. Any direction taken by the believer other than the Cross of Christ always and without fail leads to self-righteousness. If the Cross is removed from Christianity, there is nothing left but a vapid philosophy. Let it be understood that the only way to build upon the rock is to build on the Cross, which, in essence, is the rock.

"And the rain descended, and the floods came, and the winds blew, and beat upon that house," completely destroys the erroneous hypothesis of our friends who say that if a Christian has enough faith, he can confess these things away.

The implication is not that these things might come, but that they definitely *will* come, and there is no way that one with a so-called proper confession can forego these tests.

The word *beat* in the text means "struck with violence." It has reference to Satan bringing the full brunt of his attack against this house. However, with a note of finality, the Holy Spirit simply says, *"and it fell not."*

THE WORD OF GOD

The idea is that the only thing that will stand this type of test is the Word of God, and one might quickly add, the Word of God rightly divided and not twisted as Matthew 6:22-24 proclaims.

The reason the house stood was not because of its grand and glorious appointments, but simply because its foundation was sure. As we've already mentioned, many in these modern times, while viewing the storm, claim that if the individual had enough faith, such would not come, or else, there might be sin or wrongdoing that brought the storm. No! The storm has not come because of a lack of faith, but rather *because* of one's faith. Faith will always be tested, and great faith will always be tested greatly!

In truth, at times there may be wrongdoing involved, but because the house is built upon the rock, the only thing that will be destroyed about it will be the unproductive branches (Jn. 15:2).

No one can claim flawless faith or sinless perfection. Therefore, the storms are allowed by the Lord to perform a noble work of consecration in the life of the believer, although Satan's idea is to destroy. However, he will be without success!

I believe one can say without contradiction that the Bible teaches conclusively that in the spiritual sense, these floods and winds are necessary for our spiritual growth. Joseph of old, so long ago, said it so beautifully, *"But as for you, you thought evil against me; but God meant it unto good"* (Gen. 50:20).

WHAT IS THE WORD OF GOD?

Of course, the stock answer to that is, "The Word of God is the Bible." In essence, that is certainly true, as should be overly obvious; however, the story of the Bible from Genesis 1:1 through Revelation 22:21 is the story of Jesus Christ and Him crucified (Jn. 1:1-3, 14, 29).

So this means that if the believer doesn't understand the Cross of Christ, not only as it refers to our salvation, but also as it refers to our sanctification—in other words, how we live for God on a daily basis—then one cannot truthfully say that one fully understands the Word of God. He may otherwise understand many things about the Word, but unless the Cross is properly understood, all the pieces will not begin to fit together.

Regrettably, most modern believers have a modicum of understanding respecting the Cross of Christ referring to salvation, but no understanding whatsoever regarding our sanctification. And yet, 99 percent of all of Paul's teaching in his 14 epistles has to do with the Cross of Christ respecting our sanctification, in other words, how we live for God.

THE NEW COVENANT

It must be understood that our Lord, in fact, is the new covenant. That means that it's not written in stone but is rather in a person, as stated, the Lord Jesus Christ. However, the meaning of the covenant was given to the apostle Paul, the meaning of which is the Cross. So, if we want to understand fully what the new covenant actually is, which is the greatest Word ever given to a human being, we have to go to Paul's epistles.

While everything else in the Bible is the Word of God identically as that written by Paul, still, it was to Paul that this great truth was given. This means that every other writer in the Word of God in some way complemented that which Paul wrote. It is the Cross of Christ that ties together the great redemption plan.

REJECTING THE SAYINGS OF CHRIST

"And every one who hears these sayings of Mine, and does them not, shall be likened unto a foolish man, who built his house upon the sand" (Mat. 7:26).

To reject the sayings of Christ is to reject the Word of God, which should be overly obvious.

The phrase, *"And every one who hears these sayings of Mine, and does them not,"* once again proclaims the fallacy of claiming salvation when one is not attempting to obey the Word of God, but instead, is relying on false doctrine, such as:

- Once saved always saved.

- Sin is of no consequence for the Christian.

- Associating with a certain church, thinking that such saves one.

- Trusting in water baptism.

- Trusting in anything other than Christ and what He did for us at the Cross.

If one is to notice, Christ said to *"hear these sayings of Mine,"* not the sayings of other men, churches, religious organizations, etc. If whatever is taught or preached does not line up 100 percent with the Word of God, it must be rejected out of hand!

The Scripture teaches that the wages of sin is death. Christ had to die in order to pay this debt, which He did upon the Cross. There it was paid in full (Col. 2:14-15).

If you or I had died on the Cross, being an imperfect sacrifice, it would have done no good. Only Jesus, who was perfect, meaning He was not born in original sin, could provide that sacrifice, which He did.

Jesus Christ offering Himself on the Cross provided a sacrifice that God could accept and, in fact, did accept for time and eternity.

A PERSONAL EXPERIENCE

While speaking to a religious leader of a major Pentecostal denomination, he made a certain statement, which was blatantly unscriptural. I kindly said to him, "Brother, what you are saying is not scriptural."

I was speaking to him by phone, and I remember him stammering and stuttering for a few moments and finally saying, "But that is our tradition!"

It was sad. He could not deny my statement and could not buttress his with the Word of God, but he still clung to his unscriptural position.

Concerning this, Jesus also said, *"Thus have you made the commandment of God of none effect by your tradition."*

He went on to say, *"You hypocrites, well did Isaiah prophesy of you, saying, This people draw near unto Me with their mouth, and honor Me with their lips; but their heart is far from Me* (this defines the hypocrite). *But in vain they do worship Me* (worship that was not accepted by God, indicative of much of the modern church as well), *teaching for doctrines the commandments of men* (anything that adds to or takes away from the Word of God)" (Mat. 15:6-9) (The Expositor's Study Bible).

THE HOUSE BUILT UPON THE SAND

The phrase, *"Shall be likened unto a foolish man, who built his house upon the sand,"* proclaims as false every other way of salvation in the world. Irrespective of how it looks on the surface, it will not stand the test when the storms come. The Lord calls that man foolish! Regrettably, the sand builders constitute almost all of the world, and for all time!

The rock builders, even though as Jesus proclaimed, are clearly defined in the Bible, still, *"few there be who find it"* (v. 14).

It should be noticed that above ground, so to speak, both of these houses were identical. They looked alike and, in fact, were extremely similar but for one thing: the foundation. Under one was the rock, while the foundation under the other was sand.

Until the storms came, everything was rosy; however, when the storm came, and come it ultimately will, the house built on the rock stood while the one built on the sand was quickly blown away.

THE STORM COMES

"And the rain descended, and the floods came, and the winds blew, and beat upon that house; and it fell: and great was the fall of it" (Mat. 7:27).

Just as storms came upon the house built upon the rock, likewise, storms came against the house built upon the sand. However, the word *beat* in this verse is different than the word *beat* in verse 25.

As stated, there it meant "violent action," where here it means "lightly struck."

In other words, the storm against the house built upon the rock was fierce indeed, but *"it fell not,"* whereas the storm described against the house built upon the sand was of small power. Nevertheless, this house had no endurance at all *"and it fell,"* even at the beginning of the storm.

"And great was the fall of it," meant that all the elaborate religious preparation, no matter how applauded by the world, will not stand before God, i.e., His Word.

THE SERMON ON THE MOUNT

"And it came to pass, when Jesus had ended these sayings, the people were astonished at His doctrine" (Mat. 7:28).

The phrase, *"And it came to pass, when Jesus had ended these sayings,"* proclaims the conclusion of the most powerful message ever uttered on this earth, the Sermon on the Mount.

This message proclaimed the true intent of the law of Moses, and above all, laid the foundation for the new covenant that Christ would introduce. In fact, as stated, it would be the new covenant with its meaning, which was and is the Cross, that was given to the apostle Paul (Gal. 1:12; Col. 1:25-29).

"These sayings of Mine," as Christ put it, so far eclipse the wisdom of this world that it beggars description!

Without exception, everything that Jesus did was all done for you and me. In other words, He did nothing for Himself. Thankfully, what He did was accepted fully by God. To acquire the benefits of what He did, all we have to do is register faith in His person and His finished work, which is the Cross (Eph. 2:8-9).

A PERSONAL EXPERIENCE

Sometime ago, I had the privilege of reading the testimony of a dear lady who was saved by the precious blood of Jesus Christ in the country of Pakistan. As is obvious, Pakistan is totally Muslim. Consequently, she had been born and raised a Muslim, with her family quite prominent in Pakistan, actually going back hundreds of years as a part of the cultured elite. She had the misfortune of suffering a divorce and found herself lonely, heartbroken, and desperately needing help.

During this time of great trouble, being a Muslim, she turned to the Koran for solace, even though she had really never read it. The words held no meaning for her, produced no comfort, and despite her diligence to peruse the text, no solace was forthcoming.

Still desperate, her mind wandered to thoughts of the Bible, which she had not read either and, in fact, had been taught against it all her life.

Not having a Bible, through her uncle, she was able to secure a copy of the Word of God. Having never seen one before, she hardly knew where to begin but started in the book of Matthew. When she came to the beatitudes, they were a great solace to her and were the most beautiful statements she had ever read in all of her life. It seemed as though the words were alive!

Day after day she hungrily devoured the text, receiving comfort, solace, and strength.

SATAN

Nevertheless, at that time, Satan began to make his entrance. Which was truly the Word of God, the Koran or the Bible?

Even though still unconverted, she began to pray, asking the Lord to show her the truth. To be sure, an honest and sincere heart will always receive an answer from the Lord.

The Lord gently spoke to her heart, saying in answer to her request, "You have asked which book is truly the Word of God, the Bible or the Koran."

He then said, "The book which calls Me 'Father' is My Word."

A short time later, she was gloriously saved and then baptized with the Holy Spirit. Her testimony, especially concerning the manner in which the Lord led her on a daily basis, was one of the most interesting and inspiring that I've ever had the privilege to read. It was a perfect example of a false house being forsaken, with the one built on the Rock—Christ Jesus—being accepted, i.e., *"these sayings of Mine."*

ASTONISHMENT

The phrase, *"The people were astonished at His doctrine,"* proclaims their hearing words they had never heard before, especially with the spirit in which they were delivered!

Considering that these were the very people (the Jews) to whom the Bible had been given and to whom the prophets had been sent, exclusive of anyone else in the world, why were they astonished at His teaching?

They were astonished because first of all, He taught, as the next verse proclaims, with such authority and power, which was produced by the anointing of the Holy Spirit (Lk. 4:18).

As well, they had not heard the Word of God truly and honestly proclaimed, at least for the most part, in all of their lives. They were like most people presently in most churches who hear a watered-down version or no version at all.

PSYCHOLOGY

Even in many Pentecostal and Charismatic churches, which claim to believe and preach the entirety of the Word of God, still, many, if not most, proclaim a mixture of psychology and Bible, which constitutes houses built on sand.

In truth and sadly, modern humanistic psychology has become the cure-all for the ills of man. Regrettably, many, even the fundamentalists, which include the Pentecostals, Charismatics, Baptists, and Holiness, are claiming that the Bible does not hold all the answers for the behavioral problems of modern man. Therefore, they claim a wedding of the Bible and psychology constitutes the only answer.

Such drivel proclaims a total lack of knowledge of the Word of God, or of man for that matter. Such constitutes rank, raw unbelief. As such, it is sin, and decidedly so. Peter said:

> *Grace and peace be multiplied unto you through the knowledge of God, and of Jesus our Lord* (this is both sanctifying grace and sanctifying peace, all made available by the Cross), *According*

as His divine power has given unto us all things (the Lord with large-handed generosity has given us all things) *that pertain unto life and godliness* (pertains to the fact that the Lord Jesus has given us everything we need regarding life and living), *through the knowledge of Him who has called us to glory and virtue* (the 'knowledge' addressed here speaks of what Christ did at the Cross, which alone can provide 'glory and virtue'): *Whereby are given unto us exceeding great and precious promises* (pertains to the Word of God, which alone holds the answer to every life problem): *that by these* (promises) *you might be partakers of the divine nature* (the divine nature implanted in the inner being of the believing sinner becomes the source of our new life and actions; it comes to everyone at the moment of being 'born again'), *having escaped the corruption that is in the world through lust.* (This presents the salvation experience of the sinner and the sanctification experience of the saint) (II Pet. 1:2-4) (The Expositor's Study Bible).

As you read this, you now have a choice. You can accept the drivel of humanistic psychology, or you can accept the Word of God. As for me and my house, we will base our past, our present, and our future on the Word of Almighty God.

BEWARE OF THE LEAVEN OF THE PHARISEES

Once again we come back to the rock or the sand. I think it is obvious that one cannot build a house on part rock and part sand. The idea is foolish to say the least!

Any building contractor knows that if half of the foundation is insecure, such will destroy the good half as well!

That is why Jesus said, *"Beware of the leaven of the Pharisees"* (Mk. 8:15), and Paul said, *"A little leaven leavens the whole lump"* (I Cor. 5:6).

What Jesus taught was the pure, unadulterated, uncompromised, undiluted, and unassailable Word of God. Its clarity, perfection, purity, clearness, and power evoked an astonishment among the people as it will any people. That is the reason Paul said:

> *I charge you therefore before God, and the Lord Jesus Christ, who shall judge the quick and the dead at His appearing and His kingdom; Preach the Word; be instant in season, out of season; reprove, rebuke, exhort with all longsuffering and doctrine. For the time will come when they will not endure sound doctrine; but after their own lusts shall they heap to themselves teachers, having itching ears; And they shall turn away their ears from the truth, and shall be turned unto fables* (II Tim. 4:1-4).

AUTHORITY

"For He taught them as one having authority, and not as the scribes" (Mat. 7:29).

The Lord never attempts to rehabilitate the sinner, but rather does away altogether with the "old man," which refers to what we were before salvation, and then brings forth a new man—all made possible by the Cross. When the believing sinner expresses faith in Christ, in the mind of God, that person is crucified with Christ, buried with Him, and raised with Him in *"newness of life,"* i.e., the new man (Rom. 6:3-5).

That's the reason the apostle said, *"Therefore if any man be in Christ, he is a new creature* (creation)*: old things are passed away; behold, all things are become new"* (II Cor. 5:17).

The phrase, *"For He taught them as one having authority,"* refers to divine authority, which He had by the power of the Holy Spirit.

As well, every single God-called preacher filled with the Holy Spirit can and, in fact, should minister at least with a measure of that authority.

Going back to verses 21 and 22, Jesus said, *"Many will say to Me in that day."* In those verses, He declared Himself to be God, the great judge eternal. Hence, He spoke with authority, and the people felt it. None of the great prophets could use such words.

SCRIBES

The short phrase, *"And not as the scribes"* spoke of them always referring to tradition or to what some other teacher had said.

These individuals, along with the Pharisees and Sadducees, were constantly arguing over Scripture, attempting to devise tricky questions that they thought portrayed their great cleverness, but instead, only portrayed their ignorance.

They seldom told anyone how to keep the law, but instead, how not to break it. Consequently, they devised over 600 oral laws, which were tradition, and added them to the original law given by Moses. However, the laws they devised were man-devised and, therefore, carried no weight or authority because they were not of God. In fact, from the time of the Prophet Malachi to the time of Christ—a time frame of approximately 400 years—there was seldom, if ever, a *"thus saith the Lord."*

Therefore, Jesus' message was a gush of sunshine on their darkened spiritual world.

This Sermon on the Mount, and that of Luke, Chapter 6, were possibly one and the same. The Lord descended the mountain a certain distance and meeting the multitude, He re-ascended a little to a plain or level place suitable for the purpose, and there taught.

Emphasis is laid in Matthew on the necessity of a new moral birth, hence, the points about sin in the heart. In Luke, outward actions are reviewed. The distinction between "standing" and "state" becomes apparent.

Holy, holy, holy! Lord God Almighty!
Early in the morning our song shall rise to Thee,
Holy, holy, holy, merciful and mighty!
God in three persons, blessed Trinity!

Holy, holy, holy! All the saints adore Thee,
Casting down your golden crowns around the glassy sea;
Cherubim and seraphim falling down before Thee,
Who was, and is, and evermore shall be.

Holy, holy, holy! Though the darkness hide Thee,
Though the eye of sinful man Thy glory may not see,
Only Thou are holy; there is none beside Thee,
Perfect in power, in love, in purity.

Holy, holy, holy! Lord God Almighty!
All Thy works shall praise Thy name, in earth, and sky, and sea;
Holy, holy, holy, merciful and mighty!
God in three persons, blessed Trinity!

ABOUT EVANGELIST JIMMY SWAGGART

The Rev. Jimmy Swaggart is a Pentecostal evangelist whose anointed preaching and teaching has drawn multitudes to the Cross of Christ since 1955.

As an author, he has written more than 50 books, commentaries, study guides, and The Expositor's Study Bible, which has sold more than 3.2 million copies.

As an award-winning musician and singer, Brother Swaggart has recorded more than 50 gospel albums and sold nearly 17 million recordings worldwide.

For more than six decades, Brother Swaggart has channeled his preaching and music ministry through multiple media venues including print, radio, television and the Internet.

In 2010, Jimmy Swaggart Ministries launched its own cable channel, SonLife Broadcasting Network, which airs 24 hours a day to a potential viewing audience of more than 1 billion people around the globe.

Brother Swaggart also pastors Family Worship Center in Baton Rouge, Louisiana, the church home and headquarters of Jimmy Swaggart Ministries.

Jimmy Swaggart Ministries materials can be found at **www.jsm.org**.